REMEMBRANCES OF HELL

REMEMBRANCES OF HELL

The First World War diary of naturalist, writer and broadcaster
Norman F. Ellison – 'Nomad' of the BBC

Edited by David R. Lewis

Airlife
England

First published in the UK in 1997
by Airlife Publishing Ltd

British Library Cataloguing-in-Publication Data
A catalogue record for this book
is available from the British Library

ISBN 1 85310 896 0

Typeset by Phoenix Typesetting, Ilkley, West Yorkshire.
Printed in England by Butler & Tanner Ltd, Frome, Somerset.

Airlife Publishing Ltd
101 Longden Road, Shrewsbury, SY3 9EB, England

ILLUSTRATIONS

The photographs listed with a Q number are reproduced by kind permission of the Imperial War Museum. Those photographs with B.C. after the Q number are from the Barclay collection within the Imperial War Museum Photographic archive. Photographs listed as not traced have been reproduced from the Ellison diary at Liverpool Records Office.

Many of the photographs were taken in the Ypres Salient between January and May 1915 *by 2nd Lt E.C. Barclay of the Motor Machine-gun Corps. Ellison writes: 'After the war his mother gave me the negatives (223 in all), with full reproduction rights. I realized the photos were too important to remain in private hands, so I gave the films (and rights) to the Imperial War Museum in exchange for the enlargements used in this book. All troops on active service were forbidden to carry cameras, and at last Barclay was reported by one of his fellow officers. He escaped a court-martial only through the intervention of a high ranking relative in the army. His camera was confiscated, but he had been able to get his films through the censorship previously. Second Lt Barclay was killed in action in September 1915.'*

Second Lieutenant E.C. Barclay of the Motor Machine-gun Corps.

EDITOR'S ACKNOWLEDGEMENTS

I wish to thank the Copyright holders, Liverpool City Council Libraries and Information Services, for permission to publish the Norman Ellison War Diary and associated letters. Mr David Stoker, Manager of the Liverpool Records Office, and Archivist Mrs Naomi Evetts for their invaluable help in making the material available. The documents are held at Liverpool Record Office, Liverpool Libraries and Information Services.

Mr Martin Gibbs for allowing the use of extracts from *Realities of War* and *The Pageant of the Years*, the autobiography of his grandfather, Sir Philip Gibbs. Mrs Ann Thwaite and Faber & Faber Ltd for quotations from *A.A. Milne. His Life*; the Harry Ransom Humanities Research Center, the University of Texas at Austin, and Peters, Fraser and Dunlop for permission to include the letter from Edmund Blunden to his sister Phyllis. The executors of Wilfred Owen's Estate, and Chatto and Windus, for permission to reprint 'Dulce et decorum est' from *Poems* by Wilfred Owen, with an introduction by Siegfried Sassoon.

Lancashire, *Cheshire* and *Yorkshire Life* Magazines and Archivist, Mr Michael Preston, for the photographs of Norman Ellison taken by Mr Cyril Lindley in October 1971; Lt-Col M.G.C. Amlot, OBE (Retd) for information regarding the 1st/6th (Rifle) Battalion, the King's Liverpool Regiment; Wallasey Grammar School and Mr Jack Vernon for searching school records; Mr Brian Hill of *The Liverpool Daily Post and Echo* Ltd; Mr Jamie Maskey and Express Newspapers plc for the Nat Gubbins extracts.

Ms Evelyn Sawyer of the BBC Information Service; Ms J. Harvell of the British Library National Sound Archive, South Kensington; Mr Neil Somerville of the BBC Document Archive, Caversham Park, Reading; Mr David Seeney of Sunset Militaria, Herefordshire; The British Library; Cheshire County Libraries; John Rylands Library, University of Manchester; the Manchester Central Library; T. and V. Holt Associates for advice regarding the copyright of Captain Bruce Bairnsfather cartoons.

I am grateful for the help and advice received from staff at the Imperial War Museum, London, in particular Mr Roderick Suddaby, Keeper of the Department of Documents, Ms Jane Carmichael, Keeper of the Department of Photographs and Mr Paul Kemp, Licensing Officer of the Photographic Archive. Those photographs used by Norman Ellison to illustrate his War Diary, and traced in the photographic archive are credited as having come from the Imperial War Museum with individual negative numbers.

Three of the photographs are copyright Antony d'Ypres and reproduced by permission of the Design and Artists Copyright Society.

I have found it difficult to trace both the location and copyright holders of a number of photographs and cartoons that Norman Ellison used to illustrate his War Diary.

The editor is grateful to those institutions and individuals who have given him permission to use the photographs in their collections. Details of the provenance of the photographs are given in the list of illustrations. I have made every effort to contact the copyright holders of the photographs and cartoons which are unattributed but a few were unreachable. I therefore apologise to anyone whose copyright may have been infringed and would be grateful if any such individuals would contact me so that the error can be corrected in any future editions of the book.

I am greatly indebted to Mr Alan Brack for making me aware of the Ellison Archive, and for his helpful comments regarding the letters. My eldest son, Stephen Lewis, for his recent photographs taken in the Ypres area; my younger son, Philip, for his help with compilation; and to my wife, Jill, for her interest and advice.

EDITOR'S PREFACE

It has been a pleasure to edit the Norman Ellison Diary and Letters, and to make more widely available the material in the Archives of Liverpool Record Office.

Both Norman Ellison and my father Herbert Owen Lewis experienced lengthy periods of active service during the First World War, in Flanders and France, and served in the same Liverpool Territorial Battalion, the 1st/6th (Rifle) Battalion, Territorial Force, the King's Liverpool Regiment. They disembarked from the steamship *City of Edinburgh* at Le Havre on 24 February 1915. For most of the war my father served as an NCO (L/Cpl and Sgt), and was awarded the Military Medal for Bravery in the Field, France (London Gazette, 21 December 1916). He was Commissioned in June 1918 as 2nd Lt, to the 4th Bn South Lancs Regt. In later life he was reluctant to talk about his experiences so that the vivid and well observed War Diary of Norman Ellison is of particular personal interest.

The events of the First World War were of the greatest importance in shaping this century. Few of those who fought in the War and survived are alive today. One is very much aware in Flanders and northern France of the dreadful loss of life. The silent headstones in the War Cemeteries and the monuments such as the Menin Gate at Ypres, the Thiepval memorial near Albert, and the Canadian Memorial Park at Vimy Ridge, are places of pilgrimage and an acute reminder of terrible events.

An introduction to each chapter of the War Diary, in italic, has been written by the editor. Accounts from participants are revealing but by their nature partial. A chronology of the main battles of the First World War (Western Front), has been included in order to provide the historical context for events described in the diary. The photographs included in the book were the choice of Norman Ellison, with the addition of recent photographs taken by Stephen Lewis and the editor.

Crayon sketch of Arras Road. 1916. By Norman Ellison
This crayon sketch of the Arras road was made in France in 1916. It was in a frame hanging on the wall of Ellison's study in Wallasey when the house was bombed on 31 December 1940. The glass was shattered by the blast and so caused the scratches and holes seen in the picture.

CONTENTS

EDITOR'S INTRODUCTION

Norman Ellison was born at 30 Lyra Road, Waterloo, Liverpool on 26 April 1893, the first child of Frederick and Mary Ellison. He had two younger sisters, Dorothy and Winifred. Both Norman Ellison's grandfather and great-grandfather were distinguished vets. John Ellis, his great-grandfather, was Vice-President in 1860 of the Royal College of Veterinary Surgeons.

Ellison was educated at Mrs Cunningham's Private School in Waterloo, and subsequently at Wallasey Grammar School, entering the Junior School in September 1902, the family having moved across the River Mersey to Wallasey in the Wirral Peninsula whilst he was still a young boy. On leaving in December 1908, he worked in a Broker's office in Liverpool. War broke out on 4 August 1914 and six days later he enlisted in the 1st/6th (Rifle) Battalion, Territorial Force, The King's Liverpool Regiment. By February 1915 he was on active service in the Ypres area of Belgium, where he spent several weeks until wounded. He returned to his battalion at Zillebeke Lake, near Ypres in June, only to suffer an attack of trench fever in July, requiring a spell in hospital. He served in the Somme region from August to November 1915, a fairly quiet period of service during which he met the war correspondent Sir Philip Gibbs near Vaux. (The first Battle of the Somme commenced on 1 July 1916.)

The death of his mother in January 1916, at the early age of forty-eight, altered his outlook on the War. His father was seriously ill and it was likely that he would have responsibility for his two sisters. He gave up the idea of applying for a commission, for

The Ellison family in April 1914.

which he had been recommended by his commanding officer the previous November. Ellison remarks in the Diary that the average life of a second lieutenant was short. During 1916 Ellison had several periods in the trenches at Wailly, just south of Arras, returning to Ypres in September of that year. The winter of 1916–17 was very severe and he suffered from frostbite and trench foot, which in January 1917 ended his period 'on active service'.

After demobilisation in February 1920 he worked in the office of his uncle, a wholesale paper manufacturer in Liverpool. His marriage to Annie Elizabeth Wilson took place in St James Church, Carlisle on 15 September 1928. They lived in Wallasey until 1940 when they were bombed out of their house and moved to West Kirby on the Dee estuary. Annie taught Art at Dormie House School. They lived on the edge of Caldy Hill, a high ridge of heathland, birch and bracken owned by the National Trust, providing wonderful views and sunsets. Caldy Hill was the haunt of nesting shelduck from the Dee estuary, and at dusk of churring nightjars. During August one could find the striking caterpillars of the spectacular emperor moth feeding on the ling.

Annie, Norman Ellison's wife, taken in Wallasey about 1930.

In the 1940s and 1950s he produced the series of 'Nomad' books, (illustrated by Macclesfield-born artist Charles Tunnicliffe). They enjoyed a very friendly relationship, Ellison visiting Tunnicliffe and his wife Winifred, at their home 'Shorelands', Malltraeth Bay, Anglesey, in March 1955. In a letter to Nomad dated 5 April 1955, Tunnicliffe writes, 'It was nice to set eyes on your cheerful self again. Should you be in these parts again don't forget to give us another dose of the same cheering medicine.'

All of his work is written in a clear and straightforward style. His best known book, *The Wirral Peninsula*, published in 1955, went into several reprints, possibly the most comprehensive book on the area since William Mortimer's *The History of the Hundred of Wirral with a sketch of the City and County of Chester* of 1847. He spent nearly three years researching the book. As a journalist he wrote regular nature articles for the *Liverpool Echo* (under the title 'Path, Field, Sky') and for *Cheshire Life*. In his eighties he became *Cheshire Life* magazine's oldest regular contributor. He also wrote weekly 'Nature Notes' for his local paper *The Hoylake and West Kirby Advertiser*.

During the Second World War he served as a member of the Royal Observer Corps, at Hoylake in Wirral, which was important because of its proximity to Liverpool.

Norman Ellison is probably best remembered for

his broadcasts on BBC *Children's Hour* as 'Nomad' (a worthy successor to Romany, G.K. Bramwell Evans, who died in 1943). He makes the following comment in the 'Outdoors with Nomad' volume, dated 17 January 1946:

> 'Lectured to an appreciative audience at Kendal Milne's Store, Manchester. I did quick crayon sketches on paper of birds and this went down very well indeed. At the end, several people asked me for a drawing as a souvenir. Romany was a dab hand at this quick sketching business; but I regarded this only as an experiment. I shall not repeat it as I wish my lectures – and BBC programmes – entirely to reflect my own personality. I have no need to copy anyone.'

He made over three hundred broadcasts between 1945 and 1963. 'Nomad Introduces Himself' was broadcast on 16 July 1945. The 150th episode came in 1953 and the last programme in March 1963. Several of the 'Nomad' episodes were recorded for the General Overseas Service of the BBC.

All his output had the primary objective of explaining the workings of nature to the general public and particularly young people. He explained his motivation as follows:

> 'When I was a boy I spent most of my school holidays with an uncle who was a first-rate field naturalist. The love of nature and of all wildlife in those early days developed into an absorbing study which has engrossed me ever since. If I can through the media of the radio and of books, pass on this knowledge to the children of today and in some measure, be to them the guide, philosopher and friend my Uncle was to me, then I think I am doing a really worthwhile job.'

His uncle, George Ellison, had the most lasting influence on Norman Ellison's life.

'He was an architect but when he was in his mid-twenties his father died and left him sufficient to live on, and so he decided to remain a bachelor and devote himself to natural history. His vegetarianism and mild eccentricities in dress puzzled the more orthodox members of the family, but I knew them to be the expressions of a definite personality. Behind his shy and retiring manner was the determination to be himself, George Ellison, and not a nondescript human cabbage. He taught me the essentials that every field naturalist must learn; keen and accurate observation, scrupulous attention to detail and that strict integrity in the recording of any happening, so vital if the note is to have any value.'

George Ellison, N. Ellison's uncle. Photograph by N.F. Ellison.

In 1944 Norman Ellison published an article entitled 'George Ellison, Naturalist Chronicler of the Orkneys' in the *North Western Naturalist*. He explained how his uncle developed a passion for the Orkneys after a visit in 1884, returning annually for some forty years to his headquarters at Stromness. He did a great deal of original work on the flora and the Orkney vole.

In the same article, Norman Ellison remembers an occasion in 1911 when he and his uncle were collecting fleas for the leading authority, the Hon N.C. Rothschild of Tring.

> 'Bank voles were the hosts and our traps, set late at night, were inspected at sunrise. The people on the farm at which we stayed thought we were oddities to get up before 5 a.m. but when they learned we were collecting fleas – deliberately collecting fleas, then they regarded us as incurably mad.'

In 1972, at the age of seventy-nine, Norman Ellison broadcast a series about the people and places of the Wirral Peninsula. The last programme was devoted to Hilbre, a group of three small islands situated in the mouth of the Dee estuary, for which he had a special affection. Hilbre is of great natural history importance and is a Mecca for bird-watchers owing to the fact that whilst at low tide the feeding grounds around the island are uncovered, the highest tides cover everything except the islands, so that the vast flocks of birds have to crowd together on the only ground above water. Eric Hosking, the bird photographer, refers to his many visits in his autobiography. Dr Roger Tory Peterson, Lord Alanbrooke and the Duke of Edinburgh also visited the island. The sand-banks beyond Hilbre are the haunt of grey seals, the subject of a paper by Ellison and Professor J.D. Craggs for the Zoological Society of London. I visited the islands on many occasions and learnt how to identify the various wading birds such as knot, dunlin and sanderling, from the two local experts, Bill Wilson and Norman Ellison. The purple sandpiper, a winter visitor to Hilbre – between the middle of October and the end of May – was usually to be seen along with turnstone on the seaweed-covered rocks at the northern end of the island.

Norman Ellison was involved in conservation before a general public awareness of the vital importance of the protection and preservation of our fauna and flora. In 1945, learning that the local council was negotiating the purchase of Hilbre Island, he warned about the danger of excessive development. He was one of three signatories to an open letter included in 'Merseyside Plan, 1944', which eventually led to the preservation of the Ainsdale Sand Dunes Area as a National Nature Reserve. The letter mentions the rare moths and beetles, the nesting colony of terns, the unique flora of the area (including wintergreen, yellow bird's-nest and many rare orchids), the dunes as a stronghold of the vanishing sand lizard, and the marshy 'slacks' behind the dunes, the spawning place of the uncommon natterjack toad.

I became friendly with Norman Ellison in 1946, whilst I was still at school. He took a keen interest in any unusual sightings or observations that I had made and was instrumental in my joining the Liverpool Naturalists Field Club. I remember his great interest in my discovering the nest with young of a grasshopper warbler, regarded in 1947 as a scarce summer visitor to Wirral, in the grounds of Calday Grange Grammar School. He encouraged my interest in natural history. Fifty years on I still remember his amazing bushy eyebrows and the friendly reception I always received when making unannounced calls to his home on the edge of Caldy Hill.

I travelled with 'Nomad' by train from West Kirby to the BBC Radio Studios in Piccadilly, Manchester on 6 April 1946 to appear in a Children's Hour 'Request Week Nature Quiz'. This was my first visit to Manchester and Norman Ellison spent the afternoon before the live broadcast giving me a conducted tour around Manchester Town Hall, with its murals by Ford

Madox Brown, and the City Art Gallery, with its collection of Pre-Raphaelite paintings. Later at the BBC studios he introduced me to Muriel Levy ('Aunty Muriel'), Doris Gambell, Fred Fairclough and the Lancashire dialect writer Tommy Thompson, and ensured that I received their autographs. It was a memorable day.

In 1920, Norman Ellison made a start on his 'First World War Diary', but he gave it up: 'Others had written much better books than I could ever hope to write. But some years later in the mid-twenties, the rise of militarism in Germany made me think about it again.' He revisited the Ypres battlefields in 1922, and later he was able to consult the Official War diaries of his battalion, when a history of the Liverpool Rifles was under consideration. Ellison states that by November 1927 he had written some 40,000 words covering the record of the battalion from mobilisation in 1914 to the start of the Somme offensive in 1916. Due to a shortage of finance the short history of the Liverpool Rifles never materialised (see page 150). Ellison decided to use the manuscript, together with the diaries he kept (until they were absolutely forbidden just before the Somme offensive) and the letters he sent home, to complete the diary. Interested in publication he was concerned when close friends cautioned him against prejudicing the minds of young people 'before they reach an age to judge for themselves'. As a consequence between 1927 and 1934, he sought the views of many famous people of the day. The replies he received should have encouraged Ellison to finish and publish the diary, but it was not completed until 1958.

In the foreword Ellison states that the diary was not written for publication, but implies that he would not object to it being published at the appropriate time 'say fifty years hence, when, should it survive, it will enable posterity to read how war took a very ordinary young man from an office-desk and turned his well-ordered life upside down'. A letter written in 1972 to Ellison from Ronnie Pryor (who was involved in arranging the three visits of the Duke of Edinburgh to Hilbre) is interesting in that it makes clear that submissions of the diary to both the BBC and publishers were being contemplated by Ellison at that date. Pryor writes: 'It is typically generous of you to attribute the suggestion to me, but of course, the submission to your publishers has nothing whatever to do with the submission to the BBC.'

The War Diary was never published, but was microfilmed for the Imperial War Museum together with his Second World War Diary. The War Diary and Letters form a part of his eighteen volumes of memoirs. These were bequeathed in 1976 to the Liverpool City Council Libraries.

Ellison wrote a number of papers published in the Reports of The Lancashire and Cheshire Fauna Society. Two papers were written in association with Dr J.C. Chubb – 'The Marine and Fresh Water Fishes of Cheshire and Lancashire' and 'The Smelt of Rostherne Mere, Cheshire'. He also produced a revised 'Check-list of the Vertebrate Fauna of Lancashire and Cheshire' and articles on such diverse subjects as 'The Glow-worm in Wirral and Cheshire' and 'Risso's Dolphin in the Coastal Waters of Lancashire and Cheshire'.

Ellison together with Russell Anderson and Colonel 'Dicky' Wainwright organised the first reunion of the Liverpool Rifles on 24 February 1933, founding the Liverpool Rifles Association the following year. They organised a party of some forty ex-soldiers to re-visit the battlefields of France and Belgium during Easter 1935. Norman Ellison writes:

> 'The highlight of the visit was the long motor-coach tour around the battle areas we knew so well: St Eloi, Givenchy, Vimy Ridge, Arras, Wailly, Bapaume, Flers, Delville Wood, Trones Wood, Guillemont, Vaux and the Somme marshes, Suzanne and back by Bailleul and Dickebusch to Ypres.
>
> What memories the names evoked, and indeed the names were all that remained of the places we knew. Newly built villages and

churches had risen on the heaps of rubble we had lived among for so long; fields of sprouting corn hid any sign of the trenches we had defended twenty years previously. As we stood there in the spring sunshine, it was difficult to believe that the bloody shambles of the Somme battles had really taken place in the midst of this smiling countryside. But the vast beautifully kept military cemeteries showed it had been real enough and no fantastic nightmare.

I find it impossible to express the deep feelings aroused by this pilgrimage in the company of old war-time comrades. So many, so very many, of the light-hearted young men who as the First Battalion of the Liverpool Rifles had arrived in France on 22 February 1915, never returned.'

In 1930 Norman Ellison founded a gathering of friends who had served in the First World War – 'The Old Insufferables' (a reference to the Kaiser's description of the original British Expeditionary Force of 1914 as the 'Old Contemptibles'). They met each Armistice night. Four volumes of the Minutes are included in the Liverpool Records Office Archive, covering some forty-seven meetings.

President of the Liverpool Naturalists Field Club from 1942–45 and the Lancashire and Cheshire Fauna Committee from 1947–49, in 1946 Norman Ellison together with Major A.W. Boyd, MC were awarded the Charles Kingsley Memorial Medal by the Chester Society of Natural Science, Literature and Art, 'For outstanding contributions to Natural Science during the year'. He was elected a Fellow of the Linnaean Society in 1945. In 1968 he was Vice-President of the Zoological Section of the British Association Meeting at Manchester.

In his later years he suffered the sad loss of his wife Annie. Norman Ellison died in Mill Lane Hospital, Wallasey on 1 December 1976.

Articles by author and journalist Alan Brack, in *Cheshire Life* and in the *Daily Telegraph*, drew attention to the War Diary and Letters 'lying all but forgotten in the basement of the Liverpool Record Office'. Norman Ellison would have been pleased to have seen their eventual publication. His honest account of his war-time experiences will be of interest to all those who knew him through his journalism, books and broadcasts, and to later generations.

David Lewis
Mottram St Andrew
Macclesfield
Cheshire
August, 1997

PART ONE

THE WAR DIARY

LETTERS FROM THE FRONT

Dedicated to loyal friends of the First World War who came to my aid when I needed it most.

Margaret Smith-Hills
Sister, QAIMNS
and
Clem Tanner, MM
RSM, the 6th King's Liverpool Regiment

DULCE ET DECORUM EST

Bent double, like old beggars under sacks,
Knock-kneed, coughing like hags, we cursed through sludge,
Till on the haunting flares we turned our backs,
And towards our distant rest began to trudge,
Men marched asleep. Many had lost their boots
But limped on, blood-shod. All went lame; all blind;
Drunk with fatigue; deaf even to the hoots
Of gas shells dropped softly behind.

Gas! GAS! Quick, boys! – An ecstasy of fumbling,
Fitting the clumsy helmets just in time;
But someone still was yelling out and stumbling
And flound'ring like a man in fire or lime . . .
Dim, through the misty panes and thick green light,
As under a green sea, I saw him drowning.

In all my dreams, before my helpless sight,
He plunges at me, guttering, choking, drowning.

If in some smothering dreams you too could pace,
Behind the wagon that we flung him in,
And watch the white eyes writhing in his face,
His hanging face, like a devil's sick of sin;
If you could hear at every jolt, the blood,
Come gargling from the froth-corrupted lungs,
Bitter as the cud . . .
Of vile, incurable sores on innocent tongues,–
My friend, you would not tell with such high zest
To children ardent for some desperate glory,
The old Lie: *Dulce et decorum est*
Pro patria mori.

From *Poems*, by Wilfred Owen, with an introduction by Siegfried Sassoon, first published in 1920.

FOREWORD

This account of my experiences in the First World War was not written for publication. The greater part was roughly penned in the middle 1920s from my diaries and letters; a visit to the Ypres battlefields in 1922 stirred old memories. Some five years later, when a history of the Liverpool Rifles was under consideration, the official war diaries of the Battalion were obtained for me and helped me to re-live the past.

I have under-written this book deliberately as I realise how utterly impossible it is to convey the horrors of modern warfare to the reader who has no experience of them.

Compiling this book has given me a great deal of personal satisfaction. If it has any value at all, it will not be now, but say fifty years hence, when, should it survive, it will enable posterity to read how war took a very ordinary young man from an office-desk and turned his well-ordered life upside-down.

I claim no special merit for this book, literary or otherwise, save that all I have set down is true and without exaggeration.

Norman F. Ellison
30 April 1958

Rifleman Ellison. Canterbury. November 1914.

CHAPTER ONE

LIVERPOOL, AUGUST 1914

Volunteers and the outer London Defences

Britain did not, prior to the war, have a system of compulsory enlistment in the armed forces such as obtained in other European countries. There were only the Regular Army and the Territorial Force. Germany, however, possessed a very large conscript army with every male being liable for two or three years full-time service followed by four or five years in the reserve. Hence the Regular Army could be rapidly expanded when necessary.

The 1st Lancashire Rifle Volunteer Corps raised in 1859 was the forerunner of all the Territorial Infantry battalions in Liverpool. The Territorial Force came into existence in 1908. It was organised along Regular Army lines, but regionally, and was often grafted on to the local regiments. By 1914 the Territorial Force in Liverpool was well represented by the six Territorial Battalions of the King's (Liverpool Regiment). Norman Ellison enlisted with the 1st/6th Rifle Battalion on 10 August 1914. The Territorial Force was intended for home defence and men could not be ordered overseas unless they volunteered for Imperial Service. In total, 318 Territorial Battalions were raised throughout the country by splitting existing battalions in two and then recruiting back up to strength.

Field Marshal Kitchener as Secretary of State for War decided not to call upon the Territorial Force to make up the gaps in the Regular Army, but instead on 4 August 1914 appealed for volunteers for his New Army – known as Kitchener's Army. Volunteers were to be between the ages of 19 and 30 (raised to 19 and 35 by September) for a period of 3 years or until the war was concluded. The first battalion to be raised in this country as part of the 'New Army' was the 11th (Service) Battalion, the King's Liverpool Regiment.

The 17th Earl of Derby is given the credit for the idea that men who worked together (for example, in cotton, sugar, shipping etc) and met together socially, might well volunteer to serve together. This was the concept of the Pals Battalions. Towards the end of August, Lord Derby wrote to the local press and business institutions promoting the idea. He made a speech on 28 August inviting potential recruits to gather at St George's Hall, Lime Street, Liverpool, the following Monday morning, 31 August. The response was remarkable. By the following Monday Lord Derby had over 3,000 recruits, sufficient to raise three battalions of Pals. (Permission was later given to raise a fourth Pals Battalion in mid-October.) They were called the 17th, 18th, 19th and 20th Service Battalions of the King's (Liverpool Regiment).

Some 404 'Pals' Service Battalions were formed all over the country, 134 being raised in the North of England. Some volunteers to Kitchener's New Army not recruited into the Pals Battalions or the Territorials went into the Regular Battalions.

Due to a shortage of junior officers, the War Office relied initially on commissioning young men from public schools who had belonged to the OTC (Officer Training Corps). Norman Ellison criticises this practice in his Diary entry for 12 November 1915. He believed that experienced men at the front were being blocked when they applied for Commission.

In January 1916, the First Military Service Act, which replaced voluntary enlistment with compulsory military service, was passed for all single men aged 18–41. In May 1916, the Second Military Service Act extended conscription to married men, when it became apparent that the original legislation had not increased the supply of recruits sufficiently.

AUGUST 1914

It was a perfect summer of warm, sunny days, with the seaside resorts crowded and few people worrying overmuch about the ominous war-cloud hanging over Europe. Towards the end of July 1914, the threat became more real, yet the man in the street simply did not believe there would be war. The idea was preposterous and impossible. I bought a new fishing rod and made plans for a holiday in North Wales with my schoolmaster friend, Alfred Kynaston.

Suddenly there came out of the blue, the British ultimatum to Germany and then we knew it was serious. Few will forget that fateful day, 4 August 1914. The ultimatum expired at 11 p.m., and crowds waited in the streets for special editions of the papers. Sir Edward Grey was our Foreign Secretary and the scene that night as he paced his room awaiting a reply from Germany has been well described. Big Ben struck eleven and Germany had remained silent. We were at war. As he gazed through the window at a London already darkening, Grey made that prophetic comment which events were to prove so true: 'All over Europe the lights are going out and we shall not see them lit again in our lifetime.'

A great wave of enthusiastic patriotism (I can think of no better word) swept over Britain, the like of which had never been seen before or since. Any outsider would have thought we wanted war, but it was something far deeper than that. Britain was threatened and invasion was a possibility, so ordinary people rallied to the call to arms, as in the days of the Spanish Armada.

It was certainly not 'to guarantee the integrity of Belgium', nor ultra-patriotic motives that impelled me on 10 August to go to the barracks of Liverpool's crack Territorial Regiment, the Liverpool Rifles, to enlist. Rather do I think it was the chance of adventure, of getting out of a rut. I found a crowd of eager recruits waiting patiently outside closed doors. An old school friend, Jack Braithwaite, was the sentry on guard, and in front of the crowd he smuggled me through the door. The whole of Europe might be in flames but the Rifles still had a reputation to maintain. Only men of good standing were enrolled in their ranks. Major T. told us this and made no bones about it. 'My job? Where educated? What games did I play?' My answers evidently were satisfactory, so I passed the doctor, took the oath, and was given a number, 2017, a list of kit to buy out of my own pocket, and told to report next morning.

Twelve months later there was a wild scramble to keep *out* of the forces, so when I think now of those who dodged the column and of the unwilling conscripts dragged in later on, it is with an ironic smile that I recollect that I paid out of my own pocket to join the army.

Next day I bought the kit I needed out of two gold sovereigns, was fitted out at the barracks in khaki and allocated to 'B' Company. I joined it at Blackburn House Girls School, and curled up in an army blanket on the cold and hard cellar floor and tried to forget the comforts of civilian life. I was now a rifleman in 1st/6th (Rifle) Battalion, the King's (Liverpool Regiment), famed for its shooting and *esprit de corps*.

Let us pass quickly over the trials that every raw 'rookie' has to endure. On 19 August the battalion at full strength marched through Liverpool to Lord Derby's, Knowsley Park, where we pitched tents. For the first time in my life I experienced the unforgettable thrill of being one of a thousand men swinging along to the compelling strains of a band. I was proud to be a soldier.

Knowsley was a poor camp without a water supply. We shaved in hot tea or lemonade, a sticky business. My clearest memory is of running in bare feet through the dew-laden grass before breakfast, much to the astonishment of the deer. This hardened our feet and gave us razor-keen appetites that hardened our stomachs to army cooking. A week or so later we moved to Croxteth Park again under canvas. Soldiers were still a novelty to the civilian, and so the smallest detail of camp routine was performed before an admiring crowd of spectators.

Enlistment in the Territorial Force carried with it only the obligation of Home Defence, but at Croxteth we were asked if we would volunteer for Imperial Service Overseas. No pressure was brought to bear upon individuals, and it is indicative of the splendid spirit that animated all ranks, that more than three-quarters of the battalion volunteered at once.

On the last day of August, we struck camp and spent a cold, uncomfortable night huddled together on the bare ground. Next morning, whilst Liverpool was still abed, we marched down to Lime Street Station, were entrained by 8 a.m. and quickly slipped away for 'an unknown destination'. Late that night we detrained at Redhill in Surrey.

The London, Brighton and South Coast Railway had become a very important link with our Expeditionary Force in France. Throughout the day and night troop trains followed in quick succession to Dover or Newhaven. Guns, ammunition and food also poured down this vital artery, and any interruption through the activities of enemy agents would have had serious consequences. Some sixty miles of this line was entrusted to our care. Split up into small detachments, the Liverpool Rifles took up guard duties at stations, tunnels, cuttings, bridges and other vulnerable points. The work was dangerous and responsible. It called mainly for night patrols and constant vigilance. A false step meant death and during the seven weeks we performed these duties, eight riflemen were killed by trains. We slept in a variety of unusual places, such as waiting rooms, horseboxes, empty carriages, platelayer's huts and in the open. We were loaded with live ammunition and under strict orders to fire if our third challenge was ignored.

I lived in a hut made of old railway sleepers at the entrance to Merstham tunnel – a dirty, smoky place that soon made us as black as sweeps. This duty was varied with night patrols between the air-shafts ventilating the tunnel. They were situated on rough common land, pathless and lonely. I was on patrol one dark night when suddenly behind a clump of furze I saw the movement of an indistinct white patch and heard heavy breathing. A face, I thought to myself. I challenged and again. A third challenge was ignored so with my heart in my mouth I lunged at the face with my bayonet. A cow rose to her feet and made the night hideous with her justifiable protest. Another sentry challenged footsteps coming along the line in the early morning. No reply. The 'unknown' started to run. The guard turned out and after a strenuous chase captured a straying donkey. An indiscreet civilian picking his way home by an electric torch suddenly found himself inside a ring of gleaming bayonets, led by a very serious officer with drawn sword.

It was uncomfortable and exhausting work so that in the middle of October we gladly handed over our duties to the Royal Fusiliers and re-assembled at Sevenoaks as a Battalion. A brief stay there and on 29 October 1914 we reached Canterbury, the gathering point of the Liverpool Infantry Brigade where we went into civilian billets for the winter.

I was billeted with another rifleman, on a woman whose husband was serving with the Buffs in Egypt. She did not want anybody billeted on her and we were not welcome. A series of incidents brought matters to a head when we found the bolts of our rifles were full of jam. She said her child had done it. We wondered but were moved to the house of old Cooper, the cobbler. He was a character in every sense of the word. He had a dog, a lurcher, with more brains than many a human being. Very early on a Sunday morning, Cooper, the dog and I would go out poaching. I knew nothing about the game, but that dog needed no instructing. Cooper would set a net at some gap in a hedge or under a gate across the regular path of a hare, and the dog would go into the field and drive the hare into it. Then back in the keen autumn air to breakfast followed by a thorough spruce-up for church parade at the Cathedral. This amateur poaching may have been illegal and wholly reprehensible, but I enjoyed it and remain unrepentant.

We soon realised that we formed part of the Outer London defences as on our second night in Canterbury we were whisked out of bed about midnight, packed into a train and sent to Whitstable on the coast. The German fleet was out somewhere in the North Sea and there was the possibility of an enemy landing somewhere on the east coast. (Later that day the Germans bombarded Scarborough, Great Yarmouth and Gorleston.)

By the light of lanterns we dug trenches in the smooth grassy slopes of their sea-front, a wet clayey task that soon had us caked from head to foot. In the early morning we were billeted upon the surprised householders of Whitstable. Patriotism undergoes an acid test when there comes a knock on your door and without warning, you are asked to provide a billet for two strange soldiers. We waited in the road whilst Captain Wainwright, O/C 'B' Company and the billeting sergeant, Wilfred Skafte, knocked at each door and allocated one or two men there. When it came to our turn a grey bearded man with the South African campaign medals pinned to his dressing gown, an ex-army surgeon, replied to the billeting Officer's request 'I shall be proud to have soldiers in my house, Captain, provided they are clean men who will not spit upon the wallpaper'. The soldiers he knew were the regular 'swaddies' of Rudyard Kipling; fine tough fighting men but unvarnished. The war was still young and the idea of educated civilian soldiers unknown to him.

Dr C. was an eccentric who thought teetotalism a vice. On his sideboard was a large jug of whisky and milk, frequently emptied but as quickly replenished. We stayed there several days to complete the defence works on the front. On the night before we left, he asked us to invite a few of our friends to an oyster feast. Ten crowded round a table on which was a mammoth meat platter heaped high with oysters. 'There's just one thing boys, before we start,' he said, 'all the empty shells must be thrown in the firegrate.' With ten fellows pitching empty shells into the fireplace, the picture of the shambles that ensued I leave to your imagination.

We returned to Canterbury to resume the drill that was turning clerks, shop assistants – in short civilians – into soldiers. I remember vividly field days spent practising an advance in extended artillery formation by short rushes (more familiarly 'belly-flopping') across ground churned into a morass of white chalk-mud and heavily manured with decaying mussels, which brought peremptory commands from our billet landladies to 'Take your things off in the yard'. We stank like polecats.

The happenings of one night whilst on guard at our transport lines, I still remember. It was freezing hard and our tumbledown shed in the field was not even windproof. In one corner of it was a horse that had died that day, sewn up in clean sacking for burial. What was more natural than three very cold men should use that clean sacking as an extra blanket? We appreciated its warmth, and the horse felt nothing. By a happy coincidence, battalion orders next morning contained a record of the horse's death, followed by a paragraph stating that a ration of sausages would be issued to the troops the following day.

The daily distribution of rations to hundreds of men billeted, rarely more than two in a house, amongst dozens of streets, became one of those knotty problems to which no satisfactory solution was ever discovered. No doubt an ideal scheme would have embraced a subsistence or messing allowance paid direct each week to the billetors, but there were grave objections to such a course. So 'raw' rations were issued to each man, so many ounces of this, so many ounces of that. Any fine day the same scene was enacted in a dozen streets; a handcart laden with rations, and on the pavement a worried corporal and two men subdividing the meat, the butter, the bread, and even the pepper and salt, into a number of small heaps, each for a particular house.

To apportion one tin of jam between five men living in three houses, was a puzzle usually solved by the spinning of a coin. Twice we went to Sandwich to fire our musketry course on a range among the windswept dunes. The first time I was billeted in the club-house of the Prince's golf course; on the second visit in the printing works of the local newspaper. Details of those carefree days have long vanished from my mind except one. In a small and very hot hall I saw my first Charlie Chaplin film. The title escapes me but I do remember that he was a waiter who in his spare time posed as the Prime Minister of Greenland.

None of us had seen Liverpool during the five months we had been down south and with the approach of Christmas expectations of a week-end 'leave' at home ran high. It was not to be however, and our natural disappointment was dissipated in boisterous Company dinners.

With the advent of the New Year, a crop of rumours, which since the first day of mobilisation had appeared with epidemic regularity, again burst out in a severe rash throughout the battalion. 'Something' was in the wind, but what that 'something' was, each day brought forth its 'authentic' solution.

A mysterious arrival of crates at the Quartermaster's Stores contained sun helmets; somebody had seen them and at once we knew that our destination was India or Egypt. A chit had come down from brigade asking for the names of men familiar with camels, so it was Egypt for certain. Lines of communication in France; home defence on the east coast; these and other canards were swallowed and only rejected when day after day passed and nothing happened. Then the War Office set the machinery in motion.

When our black puttees went we knew something was in the wind. Always had the Sixth jealously guarded these distinguishing puttees; they had proudly answered to the name 'Blacklegs', with which the local press had christened them. A man might change cap badges and play the devil, but in his black puttees he was always conscious of belonging to the Sixth and the good name of the battalion counted for something.

Then followed an issue of paybooks, identity discs; deficiencies of kit were made good and wherever the nuts had loosened a little, they were screwed tight again. The transport scrapped their 'circus' and gloried in the possession of brand new limbers, G.S. wagons and water-carts. Rumours of draft leave persisted and eventually materialised.

Five glorious days at home and in the Liverpool which had almost forgotten the existence of the Liverpool Rifles. Soon it was Canterbury again for final inspections and farewell preparations. At last came the day, 24 February 1915. There was none of the pageantry and poignancy of God-speed in our going. At 3.30 a.m. in the chill light of a bitterly cold dawn, the battalion paraded in Wincheap for the last time. Snow was falling heavily but many of those upon whom we had been billeted turned out to bid us goodbye. The downrightness of the Lancashire character had gathered unto itself many friendships in this sleepy cathedral city, and the parting hurt.

Invisible to the onlooker was the deep undercurrent of emotion beneath the cheerful demeanour of the battalion as they flung 'Cheerio's' to the outpeering slumberers roused by the volume of our bugles in the narrow streets. Pulses beat a little faster, heartstrings gripped a little tighter for our adventure – for many the Great Adventure, had started.

Southampton was reached at last. Our transport ship, S.S. *City of Edinburgh,* well known to Liverpool eyes, was soon a hive of intense activity, winches roaring and whining as horses, mules, limbers and carts were hoisted aboard. It was a big job for town-bred men to tackle, clerks and shopkeepers who, but a few weeks ago, knew as much about a heavy draught horse or mule as they did about a dromedary. That they completed their task expeditiously and without casualty, argues that deep down in the make-up of the British, there is a horse-sense which enables them to deal with these animals, apart from experience and technical skill. As our transport sergeant summed up: 'They don't know enough to be aware of their danger; that is what saves them.'

By 6 p.m. all were safely stowed aboard and in the gathering darkness the ship cast off. Down the darkened Southampton water we nosed our way, lightless and at snail's pace, until at the entrance into the open Channel, we picked up our destroyer escort. Between decks we lay cramped and close as sardines in a tin; smoking or any kind of light forbidden; sleep well nigh impossible. Once we stopped for an appreciable time whilst our escort preyed round in great circles. The Channel had not yet been netted and enemy submarines were active.

In the greyness of early morning, cold and frosty, the harbour of Le Havre backed by the heights of the town gradually emerged from the wreaths of mist. Slowly we warped alongside the quay and quickly disembarked. We were 'On Active Service'.

CHAPTER TWO
LE HAVRE AND INTO BELGIUM

En route for Ypres, Norman Ellison was distinctly unimpressed by Flanders, particularly the flatness of the Flanders plain, the mud everywhere, and his first encounter with a Flemish farm-stead. He did, however, appreciate the hard lives led by most peasant farmers.

END FEB–MARCH 1915. FRANCE, LE HAVRE (HARFLEUR CAMP) TO FLANDERS

We had all our gear ashore by the afternoon and marched up the steep hill to Harfleur Camp: a makeshift camp of rotting tents and mud.

It was just my luck to be detailed for headquarters guard on a night of perishing cold; six of us and a prisoner in one tent. Whereas the rest of the battalion packed like sardines, some twenty men in a tent kept reasonably warm, we were half frozen. We all knew the prisoner – one of the best soldiers in the battalion – so we let him out to buy a bottle of whisky. I shudder at the thought of what would have happened had we been found out. It helped to keep us alive until morning. We entrained in cattle trucks; in each were forty men, a truss of straw, tins of biscuits, half a cheese and some tea. Add forty rifles with forty full packs and equipment, and the joke of that truss of straw 'for bedding down purposes' will be appreciated.

I shall not forget that train journey in a hurry. For twenty-one hours we jogged along, cold cramped – it was not possible to stretch at full length – and thirsty. We munched cheese and dry 'dog' biscuits, and in no uncertain language asked the authorities what blinking use raw tea was without hot water. (One truckful excepted. They had discovered a case of champagne unattended on the departure platform and 'won' it.)

Yet the feeling of high adventure and that realisation of a common lot that draws men together made everyone cheerful enough.

At last the train drew into Bailleul and a stiff and weary battalion fell in alongside the track. Borne on the keen air of that chill February morning, at times breaking through the vigorous stamping of benumbed feet, was to be heard a dull, muffled rumble. Guns. It was the growling of the insatiable Ypres Salient.

We were billeted in a school and I have never seen more men packed head to tail into such a small space. The well in the grounds was full of dead Germans; they had been in possession of the town barely three months before.

We left Bailleul on 2 March and marched twelve miles crossing the frontier into Belgium.

It was a very trying march. The roads are simply rivers of mud and full of deep holes which wet you up to the knees, unless you kept a weather eye open. At this new place Busseboom we were billeted in the loft over the shippon of an old farm – over a hundred of us – so we were packed a bit. I note from my diary:

> 'In the loft of a long shippon – 117 of us all told. Very squashy but plenty of straw and warmth. Slept like a log for 12 hours. Awakened by great shouted oaths below . . . Peeped over the side of the manger and saw a Belgian lass milking and addressing a cow with a comprehensive luridness that left no

doubt in my mind that British soldiers had been billeted here before.'

With few exceptions, the typical Flanders farmstead was a disgusting place. The single-storeyed house with a steep red-tiled roof and long straggling outbuildings form three sides of a square built around a smell – a deep expansive dunghill. The vileness of this cesspool encroaches almost up to the front door. Every window overlooks it and always does it make its presence known. Wooden shutters, brightly green, border the windows and projecting from the gable end is the revolving wooden wheel in which, on the principle of the treadmill, one of the strong nondescript dogs turns the churn inside.

The door opens direct into a large room – the kitchen, living room and bedroom all combined. The floor is of beaten earth, with the persistent rain and the constant incomings of soldiers, now surfaced with an inch of black mud. The hub around which the family life of the farm revolves is a massive iron stove set well into the middle of the room. From its top a horizontal coffin-shaped flue, on which is done the cooking, leads to a stove pipe piercing the wall. On it simmers a pan of evil-smelling grease seldom removed or emptied. Acrid fumes rise to fill the room with a bluish haze and for the moment all competing odours are vanquished. Alongside is a coloured enamel coffee-pot – always brewing, always refreshed with a pinch of coffee. The resultant coffee is very thick, black and strong, an unwholesome and unappetising drink. We pay for and tolerate it because indoors there is warmth and light, some faint echo of that civilisation we have left behind.

On the walls there are crude lithographs of religious subjects: a ghostly enlargement of son Emil serving with the Belgian Army on the Yser, a tradesman's almanac, a cheap mirror. The good wife waddles about her endless duties in a perpetual state of frowsy undress, of enormous and shapeless bulk and unbeautiful. Before the British soldier brought such undreamt of riches to the family purse, life in these Lowland countries was the long, bitter struggle of the peasant farmer. She has the hard expressionless face of those who wrestle for a living; her mate is seated by the stove puffing at a clay pipe overfilled with home-grown tobacco. Both clatter about in clumsy sabots, eminently suitable footwear for a country whose chief characteristic is mud – and more mud.

Such was the ordinary Flemish farmstead which for many months to come, with its feeds of fried eggs, chips and coffee, was to provide us with our sole taste of home life. The wonderful YMCA huts, the Divisional canteens and organised entertainments had not yet come into their own, for at that time few thought the War would last another twelve months.

Last night we left Busseboom and marched to a large town, Ypres, at present being bombarded by the Germans. At Vlamertinghe we had joined the main road from Poperinghe and taken our place in an endless procession of limbers, lorries and marching troops all bound for Ypres – the gateway to the Salient. This very ordinary road – the 'Pop' Road was, by the necessities of war, to gain a universal notoriety such as no grand boulevard in the capitals of the world could ever boast. The only main road leading rearwards from Ypres, it became the great artery which pumped an unceasing flow of life blood – ammunition, food and human beings – into the very heart of the Salient. Each in its turn, every battalion of the British and Colonial Forces must have passed between the stones of the bloody mills there which ground so exceeding small and the survivors who had trudged back along its shell-pocked pavé, had carried its ill-fame the world over.

It was gathering dusk as we marched between the ghostly poplars which sentinelled its straightness for mile after mile. It rained, as it had rained all winter, and a chill wet wind rustled the bare branches. On either hand and several feet below the road level stretched the flatness of the dreary Flanders plain; field after field of mud and sodden slime. Here and there stood a deserted farmhouse skeletonised by shell-fire; the twinkle of a shaded candle from some hidden battery position in a ditch or clump of trees; and almost encircling us – so it appeared – an endless rising and falling of magnesium flares over the Front Line trenches. Faintly in the distance was the rattle of rifle fire, punctuated by the stabbing flash and the deeper boom of a bursting shell. We tramped on . . . and on. The order 'No Smoking' was passed down the ranks and we knew we were approaching our destination.

Guides led us through deserted streets of empty houses, many collapsed in heaps of rubble, others roofless or without fronts, to our quarters in the Cavalry barracks. This had been the chief Cavalry centre of the Belgian Army in pre-war days, and a famous school of equestrianism. The place was dirty and sour smelling, but the soldier on active service asks for nothing more than six feet of dry sleeping space and a roof over his head. So we came to Ypres.

Incendie Halles d'Ypres. 22 November 1914.
Copyright Antony d'Ypres.

CHAPTER THREE

YPRES AND THE TRENCHES IN THE YPRES SALIENT

Sir P. Gibbs describes Ypres (now known as Iepers) as being the capital of our battle-fields in Flanders for the whole of the war. He went through Ypres so many times that he thought that he could find his way through it blindfold. He writes: 'Always this capital of the battle-fields was sinister with the sense of menace about'. He mentions that on most nights men were killed on the way through Ypres, 'One shell killed thirty one night, and their bodies lay strewn, headless and limbless, at the corner of the Grande Place. ..Many men were buried alive under masses of masonry when they had been sleeping in cellars, and were wakened by the avalanche above them.'

Edmund Blunden describing Ypres writes in the same vein: 'Things don't change much. Only the ruined houses get more ruinous . . . You could never find such a forbidding place. And by day, the sight of so many fine churches, convents and high houses turned into rubble is a most depressing one.'

Ypres lies on the edge of the low-lying Flanders plain with canals forming part of the drainage system, at a distance of about twenty-five miles from the North Sea, connected to it by the canalised River Yser. Because the ground is at about sea-level or below, and the sub-soil is clay, any disturbance to the drainage pattern can cause the area to become waterlogged. Consequently the low wooded slopes surrounding the plain were of great value in affording observation posts and proper trenches.

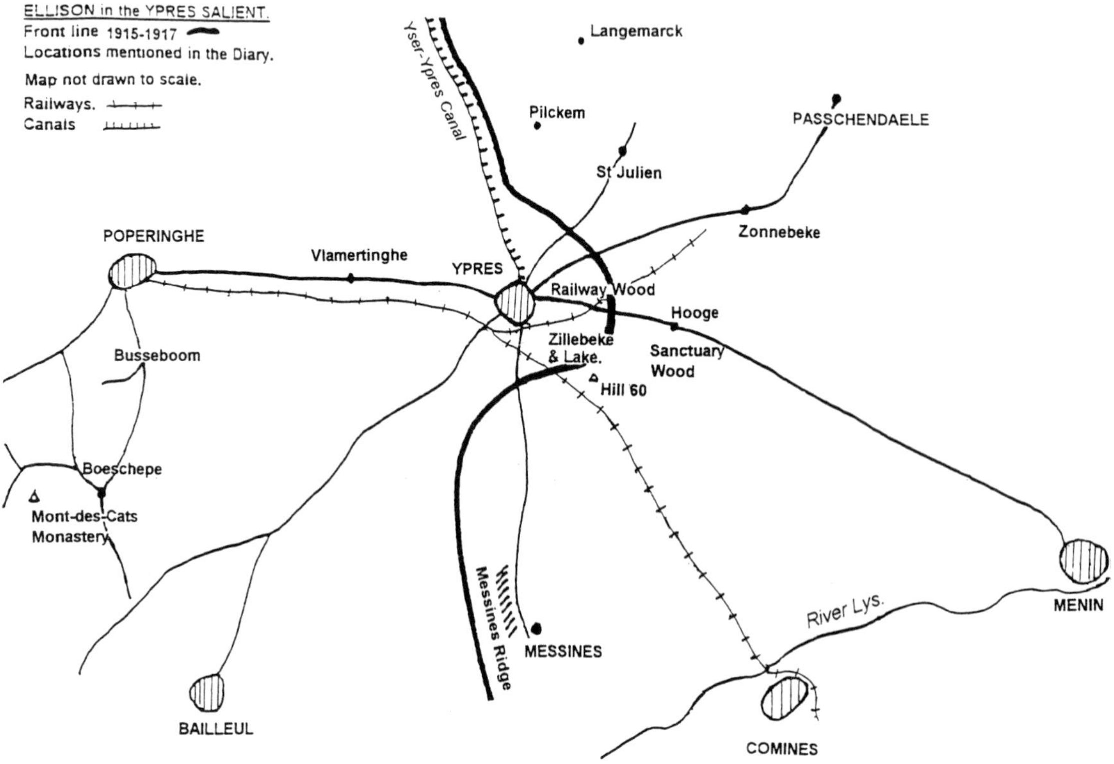

ELLISON in the YPRES SALIENT.
Front line 1915-1917
Locations mentioned in the Diary.
Map not drawn to scale.
Railways.
Canals
Yser-Ypres Canal
Langemarck
Pilckem
PASSCHENDAELE
St Julien
Zonnebeke
POPERINGHE
Vlamertinghe
YPRES
Railway Wood
Hooge
Busseboom
Zillebeke & Lake.
Sanctuary Wood
Hill 60
Boeschepe
Mont-des-Cats Monastery
Messines Ridge
MESSINES
River Lys.
MENIN
BAILLEUL
COMINES

Cloth Hall, Ypres. March 1915.Q61640. (BC.)

It reached the height of its prosperity in the twelfth and thirteenth centuries, weaving wool imported from England. In 1914, Ypres still retained its twelfth-century Gothic Cathedral and its mediaeval Cloth Hall, completed in 1304. Ypres was a natural focus for military attention due to the fact that it lay en route to the Channel ports. The town was badly damaged in the autumn of 1914 during the First Battle of Ypres. By April 1915 German shelling was gradually reducing the town to ruins. The Cloth Hall was rebuilt after the war and now houses the excellent Herinnerings Museum, Ypres Salient 1914–18.

In November 1914, the British stopped the German advance at Gheluvelt just outside Ypres. This battle in defence of the town became known as the First Battle of Ypres. The Second Battle of Ypres, 22 April 1915, famous for its use of chlorine gas by the Germans, resulted in the semi-circular bulge in the Allied lines around the east of Ypres known as the Ypres Salient. Since it was surrounded by three ridges of high ground (to the south Messines Ridge, to the east Passchendaele Ridge, and to the north Pilckem Ridge) the Germans were able to fire from all sides of the bulge, not only from the front but also enfiladed from either side. As a result it became a graveyard of British soldiers for four years.

The Menin Gate through which soldiers passed along the Menin road to the Ypres Salient, now rebuilt, but then a simple cutting with flanking stone lions, was unveiled by Field Marshal Viscount Plumer on 24 July 1927, and commemorates the British and Commonwealth soldiers who died in the Ypres Salient before 16 August 1917 and have no known graves. The Last Post is sounded beneath the Menin Gate every night, and this has been done regularly since 11 November 1929, with a break during the German occupation, 1940–44.

The British Government awarded the Military Cross to the Burgermeister and Residents of Ypres on 29 January 1920.

Trench Conditions

Whole sections of trenches would sometimes collapse due to the action of frost and rain. The cold and wet conditions experienced in the trenches caused problems such as 'Trench foot', painful swelling of the feet accompanied by blistering and ulceration, which in severe, untreated cases may go on to gangrene. During the winter of 1915 there were over 400 cases in one battalion of the 49th (West Riding) Division, and other battalions suffered as much. Norman Ellison contracted Trench foot in the very severe winter of the following year, 1916. More recently Trench foot affected troops engaged in the 1982 Falklands War.

Cathedral, Ypres. February 1915. Q61644. (B.C.)

Cathedral, Ypres. Recent photo by Editor. 1996.

Cloth Hall. Recent photo by Editor. 1996.

Menin Gate, Ypres. Recent photo by Stephen Lewis. 1996.

5 MARCH 1915, YPRES. THE CAVALRY BARRACKS

It is only two miles behind the actual firing line and as I write I can hear shells whistling overhead and the crash as some house is struck. The town itself is practically in ruins, yet many of the inhabitants are still here. They live in their cellars or dig themselves holes – dug-outs – in some bank.

You have to see the damage done by a 'Jack Johnson' to realise its power. One fell some weeks ago at the rear of these barracks completely destroying a house and making a crater quite twenty feet wide and fifty feet long, to expose the underground River Yperlee. In this stream we wash ourselves and water the horses; it is such an odd sight to see fellows having a dip on a few planks in the middle of the street.

I was on a fatigue party for sandbags this morning and had to go to another part of the town, when the Germans opened fire. We could hear the shrapnel playing on the roofs and the children screaming as they bunked to their underground burrows. We saw men looting among ruined houses for gas-fittings, pipings and other odds and ends. I suppose on this game you become something of a philosopher, the odds being enormous against a shell falling on the *exact* spot where you are. I have come in contact with a lot of the Regulars and they are fine fellows, calm, self-possessed and with a humorous and laconic contempt for the foreigner and his ways that appeal to me immensely. I also have a smile to myself when I think of those pictures 'Drawn by our own Artist', of a line of our men immaculately rigged-out attacking something or another. I wonder if

Ypres. Vault under the street, exposed by shelling, containing the River Yperlee — draining Zillebeke Lake and maintaining the level of the moat at the Lille gate.

there is a fighting man in the British Army out here who could parade for a strict inspection? Most of us are in all sorts of ragtime costumes and plastered with mud and slush from head to foot.

In the hard fighting of the previous November, the city had suffered severely and since then scarce a day had passed without its dose of shell-fire. The Cathedral and Cloth Hall – gems of mediaeval architecture – had been badly knocked about. The roofs had gone and the rain poured in on the mural frescoes and paintings which had been their pride. Many of the inhabitants who had fled before the first enemy invasion had returned to their homes and shops and did a roaring trade with the troops. Eggs, bread (there was no army issue at this time), tinned fruits, postcards, chocolate and beer tempted us to spend our few francs. In the Rue de Lille was a restaurant run by two enterprising women, who in the old days had catered for the social functions of the local gentry. There could be obtained an excellent dinner and good wines. (The red silk blouses worn by the owners is an unimportant detail which has remained in my memory.) One remembers the butcher's shop facing the Cloth Hall, whose window was ornamented with 'dud' shells gaily bedecked with entwined ribbons of the Allied colours. (There came the day when a live shell fell among those 'duds', and the patriotic pork-butcher had the honour of a semi-military funeral.)

Before breakfast we would run over from the barracks to a *pâtisserie* in Rue de la Station, where could be obtained the most ravishing hot chocolate and confections. One morning the shop was shut and rumour had it that the proprietor had finished up with his back to a stone wall, owing to the matter of some signalling apparatus hidden upon his roof. The spy mania was acute in those days and justified. Spies were everywhere and many were the dodges they employed to get their information to the enemy. We heard of a dog which had been observed making several trips to and from the German lines. It was shot and discovered to have a false skin laced over its real one, the messages being carried in between. Another time there came instructions to take to the nearest guard-room any nun who looked in any way suspicious, for enemy agents had been caught in that garb. But for the genuine nuns who clung to ruined Ypres until they were ordered to leave, we had the warmest admiration. No matter how heavy the shelling they would go out into the streets and attend to the wounded, soldier and civilian alike.

The Irish nuns had a convent in Rue Sainte Elizabeth, which had been turned into a temporary hospital. One morning I had been there to take some letters to a sick man from my platoon, when there came the whine and crash of a shell near by. I slid into the nearest doorway to wait until the little 'hate' was over. Suddenly I felt a hand on my shoulder and a hooded sister said 'English soldier come please'. We went down the road and carried into the convent a pitiful moaning bundle with a red-stained pinafore. I like to think that little girl lived. I fancy she was more frightened than mortally wounded. So could many a soldier tell of

Boiler set on fire by shelling, near Ypres, March 1915. Q61552. (B.C.)

Sandbagged entrance to the Ramparts. Ypres. Q. 28949.

his help sought by some sweet-faced woman in a nun's severe garb. They were noble women.

Several men of the battalion, noticing the erratic movements of a weather vane surmounting a church steeple on a calm day, brought their rifles and shot it off. The Germans held the high ground overlooking the city and during daylight every movement in the streets must have been visible to them.

But all this atmosphere of 'business as usual' was a sham, a pretence. In the moat and underground waterways of the city, in the cellars of the fallen houses, rotted the dead bodies of men and women, and the occasional screech of a shell and the crash of a falling building was a constant reminder of what had been and could be again.

It now becomes necessary to take a brief review of the situation existing in the Ypres Salient when we joined there the 15th Infantry Brigade, composed of the Regular battalions of the Bedfords, Cheshires, Dorsets and Norfolks.

The city of Ypres lay as it were, in the centre of a shallow bowl, two-thirds of whose rim, the high ground, was in enemy occupation. Always was the advantage of ground with him. Furthermore so deep was the bite into his lines that he could enfilade our trenches with rifle-fire and even bring his artillery to bear direct upon our rear. There was not even partial security anywhere in the Salient.

Everywhere the ground was a churned up morass of knee-deep mud. In places the slime seemed bottomless, and woe betide the man who

A billet near Hooge set on fire by shelling. Q61612. (B.C.)

fell in. His chances of extricating himself unaided were small. Thousands of deep shell-holes filled with water caused by projectiles of a size such as had never been used before, except against fortifications, pitted the countryside; terrible traps for the unwary.

When we joined the Regulars in the line, except for their unquenchable determination and optimism, they were scarcely recognisable as British soldiers. It was now early March 1915 and since the beginning of the war in the previous August, without rest, without relief or the hope of it, these grim and splendid men, caked with mud to the eyes, had faced the enemy and fought him to a standstill. Long ago had the seeming limit of human endurance been passed, but still they hung on against an enemy greatly superior in numbers and overwhelmingly so in artillery. We had no reserve troops and there was a criminal shortage of artillery ammunition. (In the Salient each gun was severely rationed to three shells a day. Only in the direst circumstances could this amount be exceeded.) Our heavy artillery comprised a few naval 4.7s and two nine-inch guns. Rifles and invincible courage, nothing else, held Ypres, the key to the Channel ports.

The Front line had not yet developed into the highly organised trench system of later days – named, numbered and with signposts at every corner. Here we had a series of non-continuous trenches, hastily dug when the opposing armies had faced each other in their attempted outflanking movements to the northward. Water appeared within two feet of the surface and there were more sand-bag breastworks than deep-dug trenches. Reserve lines and the long communication trenches zigzagging to the rear for a mile or more, had not yet appeared. Troops were too few and too exhausted to be spared for such immense tasks.

Trench relief was carried out in the darkness by

Front line trench, Ypres Salient. March 1915. Q61595. (B.C.)

small parties crossing open ground until you came to the support line. Frequently you were under direct fire and so every time Jerry sent up a flare you stood quite still or, if he opened fire, threw yourself flat on the ground and waited until the flare burnt itself out. For a minute or so you were semi-blinded with the brilliance of the light. I remember on a particularly dirty night being one of a relief party, when up shot a flare and a machine-gun opened out. I went flat in the mud alongside another fellow. When the flare had fizzled out I said to him 'Come on', but he did not reply. Thinking he had been hit I got hold of his arm to help him up when . . . it was a French Poilu who had lain out there for months. Lewis guns were unheard of; machine-guns were few and far between; the lines on either side were crammed with men standing shoulder to shoulder.

From a spot along a hedge at the rear of the International Trench (so called because French Belgian, British and German troops had held, lost and retaken it, time and time again) it was possible to look down the two lines towards the Bluff and to see on the one side the spiked rows of German helmets and on the other, the flat caps of the British. This International Trench, an advanced trench, was a good example of the close nature of the fighting. The Germans held one half and the British the other, with only a single sandbag block in between them. One of our Officers, wishing to satisfy his curiosity raised himself by his hands and looked over the block. By coincidence a German Officer did the same at that moment and the two in astonishment glared into each other's faces.

Dead bodies, in varying stages of putrescence, lay about everywhere, unburied from the fighting of the previous autumn. It was not possible to dig without encountering corruption. The French, original makers of these trenches, had built some of their dead into the parapets and parados of the trenches, so that in places the living sheltered behind the dead (logically a sound proceeding but to the sentimental British it seemed disgusting). Hands polished by the constant friction of passing khaki to the texture of old ivory projected from the trench wall; legs, boots . . . Repairs to the trench walls was a sickening job jibbed at by everyone.

There were no organised cooking arrangements in the Front line. Each man had his raw rations – biscuits, bully beef, cheese, jam, bacon, tea and sugar – and he had to make shift for himself as best he could. There were iron braziers and wet coke to be had, but these were of little use. The British Army lived on tea, all hours of the day and night, and bacon cooked over candles or weird lamps made of rag soaked in bacon fat.

Most of the trenches were knee-deep in water with no bottom boards – duckboards – as we called them later on, to prevent the involuntary step into a waist-deep hole, or the side-slip on a clayey bottom curved by the passage of hundreds of feet. The trench sides oozed a liquid mud until our tunics and greatcoats became saturated and intolerably heavy. As the heat of the day increased the sodden accumulation of our night-time journeyings on fatigue and working parties dried out and stiffened into an enveloping sheath. Unwashed, unshaven, and plastered with mud from head to foot, any British infantry of those days, slowly plodding a watery way through the trench rearwards for a rest, could well have been compared to a herd of great shaggy bison returning from their mud wallows.

Trench life in the daytime was a boredom, a tedious exasperating wait broken only by spasmodic shelling or the occasional crack of a sniper's rifle. For a few hours you crept behind a hung ground-sheet into a low cramped hole scooped out of the trench wall and in the sleep of utter physical exhaustion, forgot the degradation of human life outside.

With sunset there came 'stand to' for an hour, for during this period and the hour of similar half-light before dawn, surprise attacks were most likely to be made. The elaborate wire entanglements properly staked and interlaced, many yards wide, had not yet appeared in the Salient. Our barbed wire defences consisted solely of a few 'knife rests' pitched over the parapet. With darkness the trench was galvanised into life: the scuttling night life of so many rats along their burrows and runs. Sentry duties, sandbag repairs both outside and inside the trench, ration parties, carrying fatigues, a hundred and one duties were performed under the cover of night. No man was idle; there was rest for none.

The volume of rifle-fire increased, the rat-tat-tat of machine-guns was added to the din. Shells, for the most part German, whined in luminous streaks overhead or burst upon the trench. At frequent intervals magnesium flares soared from the opposing lines and for a few seconds picked out No-Man's land with uncanny clarity. Starting far distant up the line would come the never forgotten sound of 'rapid fire' growing in intensity as it came nearer, sweeping down like a prairie blaze and as contagious, until suddenly you found yourself amidst an inferno of sound, pumping lead as fast as fingers could load, and pulling the trigger into the blackness ahead. This 'wind up', due to the panicky desire of nerves tensed to breaking point to 'do something', would pass on and gradually die out in the distance.

The day's casualties (German snipers were taking a heavy toll for there were very few periscopes to be had and sentries *would* look over the parapet in daylight), had to be evacuated, the wounded to the advanced dressing-station, the killed to the nearest convenient spot for burial. There were few jobs more heartbreaking than the negotiating of a dead-weight stretcher through the windings of a greasy trench. It called for great physical endurance and a stout heart, especially if the burden was still conscious.

With the first chill streaks of dawn, work would cease and all would 'stand to' the firing step. The rum issue, a tablespoon for each man, dished out during this hour before daylight, infused new life into men wearied beyond words. When daylight was fully established, you cleaned your rifle and if not on sentry duty, slept for an hour.

Another day had begun, and thank God you were still alive.

On 7 March we left the Cavalry Barracks as darkness fell for our first spell of Front line duty with the 1st Bedfords for instruction. Guides were sent down from the trenches to meet us, but they kept losing their way and we took five hours to do just a little over two miles. It was an exhausting journey through knee-deep mud; at one time we were hopelessly lost and found ourselves actually between the German lines and our own.

Early next morning five of us were round a brazier in the Front line, frying some bacon, when a shell exploded among us. Clarke was killed outright; Fisher so badly wounded that he died an hour or two later; Furniss was wounded too. Frank Evans and I were knocked out for several minutes but did not receive a scratch. It was a pretty grim introduction to trench life. Poor Fisher had the top of his head sliced off like an egg and I was bespattered with his brains. I wanted to be physically sick, so did Frank Evans, but we quickly realised that would never do, so we carried on. I cleaned myself up a little and managed to swallow some breakfast. It was one of our shells too, a Belgian battery firing short.

During the day it snowed and the trench became a quagmire. The Dorsets relieved us that night and again it took us five hours to traverse the two miles to Ypres. We turned in as we were, wet through and tired out; a generous issue of rum alone saved us from chills and worse complications.

9 MARCH 1915, THE CAVALRY BARRACKS, YPRES

We have just arrived back from a 24-hour spell in the trenches caked with mud. It is exceedingly cold there; snowing in fact and so we are glad to get back to the comparative comforts of a civilised life. Before we go in, we smear our legs and feet with a fatty substance – 'anti-frostbite' it is called and it keeps out the cold to a certain extent. It smells abominably of whale oil, but we are glad of it.

11 MARCH 1915

We were out road-mending all yesterday clearing away mud about a foot in depth and then making a solid foundation out of faggots and brushwood. It was hard work and after twelve hours at it, most of us were fagged out. We have earned very high praise from the Regulars themselves for our coolness under fire. I was rather surprised myself because as a rule, new regiments are inclined to be nervy.

15 MARCH 1915

We have been here eleven days now – practically in the firing line all the time – either in the trenches or else carrying ammunition up to them. The last named is a terrible job as the boxes weigh 80 lb and are slung on a pole between two men. You have to go in the pitch dark absolutely cross-country, with the result that you spend half your time falling into ditches and water-filled shell-holes and then running like hell until you catch up to the rest of the party.

We have all cut our greatcoats down to peajacket size as we found that they used to drag in the mud and then weighed us down like ton weights. The more I see of the Regulars, the more am I convinced what magnificent fellows they are; absolutely nothing will make them downhearted.

After several spells in these trenches, we were relieved on the last day of March by the Queen Victoria Rifles and marched back to hutments at Vlamertinghe. Military science had not yet advanced to the stage of providing waterproof cover for the troops and these Nissen huts leak abominably. Here too, we made our first acquaintance with bombs.

The Germans with characteristic thoroughness had anticipated trench warfare and were supplied with bombs of a fairly efficient type. We had practically none. No doubt all in good time, the wheels at home would commence to turn, but in the meantime it became necessary for us to have some sort of reply. Several of us were instructed in the art of making jam tin bombs. An empty jam tin, a primer of guncotton, a detonator, some fuse and as many stones, iron and old nails as could be crammed in, went to the make-up of this wonderful bomb. The burning of the fuse was always an unknown factor and there was more than considerable risk attached to the lighting and throwing of these bombs. Frequently it would happen that a bomber uncertain whether the fuse had gone out or not, would not stop to investigate such a delicate matter, but would pitch the bomb

The Liverpool Scottish billeted in the Infantry barracks, Ypres. March 1915. Q61570. (B.C.)

Motor machine-gun unit building a dug-out in reserve line, Ypres Salient. March 1915. Q61594.

Motor machine-gun unit (Scott motorcycle) firing at aeroplanes. Q61576. (B.C.)

The field Postcard.

NOTHING is to be written on this side except the date and signature of the sender. Sentences not required may be erased. If anything else is added the post card will be destroyed.

I am quite well.

~~*I have been admitted into hospital*~~
~~*sick*~~ ~~*and am going on well.*~~
~~*wounded*~~ ~~*and hope to be discharged soon.*~~

~~*I am being sent down to the base.*~~

I have received your *letter dated* ____ ~~*telegram*~~ ,, ____ *parcel* ,, ____

~~*Letter follows at first opportunity.*~~

~~*I have received no letter from you*~~
~~*lately.*~~
~~*for a long time.*~~

Signature only. Norman Ellison

Date 2 April 1915

[Postage must be prepaid on any letter or post card addressed to the sender of this card.]

(25225) Wt.W3497-293 1,760m. 3/15 M.R.Co.,Ltd.

The field postcard was one of the really bright ideas the army had. It enabled the soidier to keep in touch with home when letter writing was not possible. As names of places were forbidden in all correspondence, we let those at home know our whereabouts by spelling the name with light dots over the necessary letters. I have ringed the dotted letters - YPRES. So far as I know the authorities never discovered this simple scheme. These cards were not rationed.

into the enemy trench. Sometimes it would be returned, lighted, with unpleasant results to the original thrower. This nasty habit of returning our bombş became so regular, that at last some ingenious mind thought out a means of stopping it. He fused a bomb with instantaneous fuse, stained black instead of scarlet, and threw it unlighted into the enemy trench. After that the enemy gave 'dud' British bombs a wide berth and none came back.

5 APRIL 1915. CHATEAU ROSENDAAL (OFF THE LILLE ROAD). A FEW DAYS SPENT IN SUPPORT

The Château is a fine building with wonderful stables but it is all wrecked. The owner is called Bloc, a breeder of racehorses. The place had been thoroughly looted with only larger articles of furniture left. Priceless carpets have been nailed over windows to prevent lights being seen. The Château is quite near the line so that we are not allowed to stir out in daylight since we are under enemy observation. I noted a splendid Grandfather clock battered with pieces of shell. The boys have just unearthed a piano in playable condition, but the lid has gone for firewood. A sing-song is in progress with a shell or two coming over in the grounds, not far off.

I find it difficult to believe that today is Bank Holiday and that many people will be enjoying themselves whilst we poor devils are slogging into it.

On Good Friday I attended an open-air service by the Bishop of London. He is a fine man and talks as if his audience were men, not the sinful iniquitous wrecks the prigs at Canterbury Cathedral evidently took us for. He is a racy speaker, witty and looks like a prosperous bookie.

In the evening I went to a Cinema show in an old barn. It was entertaining, although the boom of the guns and the squealing of the pigs at the other end of the barn rather drowned the efforts of the pianist.

CHAPTER FOUR

HILL 60 AND THE SECOND BOMBARDMENT OF YPRES

Hill 60, so named from its 60 metre height, was a low ridge of earth 250 metres in length, thrown up from the spoil during the excavation of a cutting for the Ypres–Comines railway in the previous century. It was prominent in the flat Flanders countryside and provided a useful observation post, commanding views in all directions. It was the hinge at the edge of the Salient where the high ground swung south. It was bitterly contested. The Germans had captured it from the French on 10 December 1914. In February 1915 the British, who took over the sector from the French, decided that because the Germans could completely overlook our defences, it was vital that Hill 60 should be recaptured.

A special group of Sappers from the Royal Engineers (171st Tunnelling Company) were recruited by Lt-Col Sir John Norton Griffiths, who was attached to the staff of GHQ to organise and initiate Tunnelling Companies. The 'Clay-kickers' as they were known included former Liverpool and Manchester navvies who had dug sewers for his civil engineering firm. Over a period of some months they drove three shafts into the Hill in order to lay six mines under the German Front line. It became a race when it was realised that the Germans were engaged in the same task. In fact on one occasion the tunnellers broke through into a German shaft.

Each tunnel forked right and left just before reaching the German Front line. The tips of these arms were widened to house the mines which were

Hill 60
Ypres-Comines Railway
Zwartleen
Road Bridge
Southern Armagh W
Taken from the Dump, Verbranden Mole
Sheet 28.I. 29.c. 2.4. Direction E. by N. to S.S.E.

Merckem (north of Ypres). Copyright Antony d'Ypres. 190418.1

Hill 60. 10 April 1915, a week before it was blown up. At that time my company was holding the trenches on the right of the picture. Q37385.

laid in waterproof boxes and wired back to plunger exploders. The tunnels were then blocked with sandbags to ensure that the blast went forwards towards the Germans. At 7.05 p.m. on 17 April 1915, the mines containing over 10,000 pounds of explosive were fired. As they detonated the ground shook and with a deafening roar and crash, clouds of earth and stones rose from the summit of the hill scattering debris over a wide area. At the same time the British, French and Belgian artillery opened fire. The infantry (Royal West Kents) charged up the hill and occupied the crest. The mines had demolished the top of the hill, with craters in place of the trenches.

Vigorous counter-attacks were mounted by the Germans with a very heavy artillery bombardment, a hand-grenade attack and a bayonet charge. The King's Own Scottish Borderers were sent up Hill 60 in order to relieve the Royal West Kents but at that moment the Germans launched a further counter-attack. Fifty per cent of the officers and men of the Royal West Kents were casualties.

The whole crest of the Hill 60 was eventually taken by our troops (the Duke of Wellington's Regiment and the 2nd King's Own Yorkshire Light Infantry) but only after furious hand-to-hand fighting, with bombs being hurled at a few yards range. There were over 1,500 casualties.

The Germans used chlorine gas on 5 May to retake

the Hill and held it for the next two years.

The final destruction of Hill 60 took place in May 1917 when the Second Army, commanded by Sir Herbert Plumer, undertook to capture the Messines Ridge. The key factor in the success of the operation was the simultaneous explosion of nineteen mines under the Ridge, including Hill 60 at its northern end. Twenty galleries were driven for almost 8,000 yards under the German Front line trenches by British, Australian and Canadian tunnellers. It took more than six months to dig the shafts, one of which was 2,000 feet long.

The mines with enormous explosive power were laid in readiness for the assault, and were detonated at 3.10 a.m. on 7 June 1917, with devastating results. The explosions were followed by a British artillery bombardment of over two thousand guns. It is thought that at least ten thousand German soldiers were either killed or buried alive. The Germans withdrew from Messines four days later. The two Hill 60 craters can still be seen today.

The Germans recaptured Messines in April 1918 before the British finally regained the sector in September of that year.

14 APRIL 1915. IN A TRENCH OPPOSITE HILL 60

We are up at the trenches for eight days (two days in trenches and then two days in dug-outs), a couple of hundred yards behind the firing line. The country round here is beginning to look fresh and green and very spring-like. For the most part it is undulating with many slight rises, hardly as high as Bidston Hill.* On nearly every one there is a windmill which, unless the artillery has battered it to a wreck, is generally working.

The part where we are is exceedingly well wooded; virgin forest of small pines some forty feet high. We cut down thousands of them and put them to all sorts of uses: making roads over swampy places; building log huts *à la* cinema style and so on.

*** Bidston Hill in Wirral is 231 ft high.**

Dug-outs in woods in front of Blauepoort Farm, to right of the Cutting, Hill 60, Ypres. Q61566. (B.C.)

A British Pill Box on Hill 60. Recent photo by Stephen Lewis. 1996.

The Rifle Pits before Sanctuary Wood, Ypres.

There is practically no pasturage, every available spot being cultivated either under crops or as hop fields (any amount of the latter). The soil is rich and very heavily dressed with manure, hence the stringent precautions we take against tetanus. The features that strike you most are the complete absence of hedges and the lines of tall, straight poplars bordering every main road for miles. The people have as much idea of the general rules of sanitation as a gargoyle and are filthy and untidy in dress and everything else. Welsh farms are models compared with the majority of these. Anyway what can you expect from a people who pin their faith to sloppy, slithery sabots? Give me neat Lancashire clogs every time. The peasants speak Flemish of course, a disgusting grating language to the ears and ninety per cent do not understand French. If you enter a farm, it is generally the youngsters you talk to for they get a smattering of French at school.

On 17 April we were huddled in dug-outs some hundred yards behind the Front line. 'Dug-outs' is a misleading description when one thinks of the deep concrete and timbered shelters constructed later on. These were shallow holes scratched in a sloping bank, covered with a groundsheet and proof against nothing heavier than rain. Two or three of us crawled into each for mutual warmth and slept the deep sleep of physical exhaustion.

At mid-day we were turned out and ordered to reinforce the 1st Norfolks in the Front line, as a major operation was coming off that night. All rifles were cleaned and oiled; between each two men a full box of ammunition was placed. In the late afternoon we were told that Hill 60 was to be blown up that evening. The hill was only an insignificant mound – the spoil bank from the cutting of the Ypres–Comines railway – some 200 yards away on our left front.

It was a calm spring evening, quiet with desultory rifle-fire here and there. We waited, tense and ready for 7 p.m. Three deep rumbling roars and the seven mines beneath the hill were exploded. The crest lifted up bodily to dissolve into dense pillars and spurts of black smoke and dust. 'Keep close into the parapet to escape falling debris' had been our orders and we crouched low into the base of the sandbag wall. Immediately 'bang bang bang!!!' ripped out a battery salvo. It was the signal hundreds of gunlayers had been awaiting. A sound that grew louder and louder rose from the hissing rush of escaping steam to a screaming roar which seemed to fill the sky with its concentrated volume. Then when it reached a pitch beyond which it seemed impossible to rise, it broke in a terrifying rolling C–R–R–RASH, which rocked the ground on which we stood. The German lines were quickly hidden in smoke and yellow lyddite fumes, through which sandbags and pieces of debris could be seen spinning into the clearer air above. The enemy soon recovered from his surprise and laid down a heavy shrapnel barrage on our trench, but his ranging was poor and we had few casualties.

As night closed down, our bombardment became intensified. Looking over the back of the trench the dark was pricked by innumerable gun flashes. From every point in a semicircle came the visibly luminous trails of white-hot shells converging overhead upon the enemy lines. In the midst of a tumult, which benumbed all clear thought, there came the exultation of knowing that these were *our* guns and *our* shells. We were paying them back with interest for the shelling we had endured without retaliation for months past.

We spent most of that night flat upon the parapet, firing until the barrels of our rifles became red-hot and blistering to the touch. All night through a man went up and down the trench with a can of oil which he poured on the open breeches. It boiled and fizzled and made the trench smell like a fish and chip shop. There was no barbed wire protecting us, and so our job was to keep Jerry in his trenches.

All next day the enemy plastered the remains of the Hill with heavy explosives. We could plainly see the Germans lining up for the attack on the slopes of 'The Caterpillar', another mound to the rear of the Hill. A detachment of the Motor Machine-gun Corps had come up to our trench and found the masses of field-grey, moving up steadily as if on parade, an easy target for their guns. They mowed them down and cut lanes through their ranks, but the survivors continued to advance. Presently we saw them appear in ones and twos over the rim of the crater left by the explosion, and come to hand-to-hand grips with the Cameron Highlanders holding the Hill. Those Germans were brave fighters.

The following days, the 18th and 19th of April, were lively too, with the enemy bombardment far heavier than ours. Our ration parties had experienced great difficulty in getting through supplies and there was a shortage of drinking water in the trench. We took water from shell-holes, strained it through a handkerchief, boiled it and disguised its taste and colour with a handful of tea. On both afternoons we had our first experience of tear-gas shells. The irritation and weeping of our eyes was so distressing that, leaving a few sentries behind, we retired for a time to a reserve trench some one hundred yards to the rear.

THE SECOND GREAT BOMBARDMENT OF YPRES

On 19 April the second great bombardment of Ypres commenced. High above our heads we heard the passage, like the rumbling of a railway train, of enormous 17-inch howitzer shells. As they burst amongst the buildings of the town, reddish clouds of brick-dust, hundreds of feet high, shot into the air and slowly expanded into a heavy pall over the doomed place. The damage caused by these large shells was enormous. A few weeks later I was with a party in Ypres looking for unbroken mirrors to cut up into periscopes. The streets were pocked with shell craters forty feet across and as many feet deep. Whole rows of houses had collapsed like a pack of cards; many had the whole facade torn off to expose the interior, floor by floor, like some tragic doll's house with a hinged front.

Ypres Street scene. April 1915.

The bombardment had been expected and the battalion details (HQ, Signals, Aid Post and Quartermaster's Stores) in the town were ordered to find shelter. Our adjutant, whilst making enquiries about suitable cellars, was told of the great tunnels under the ramparts of the town, constructed some two hundred years ago by the famous engineer Vauban as powder magazines . . . These casemates, the size of railway tunnels were found filled with rubbish and apparently forgotten. We cleared them out and no better shelter could have been devised. The solid masonry and the depth of covering earth made them practically shell-proof.

The first shell fell among a bunch of children at play and killed fifteen of them. Thereupon a panic ensued and terror-stricken refugees, their few most precious belongings trundled upon a barrow, crowded into the bottleneck of the town and streamed along the Poperinghe road, the only route to safety. Shells dropped amongst them. Terrible were the sights witnessed by the battalion details as under the untiring leadership of our Medical Officer, Major Graham Martin RAMC, they organised search parties to help the wounded and dying in the streets, soldier and civilian alike. With wonderful courage they worked day and night, each sortie from the casemates a succession of narrow shaves. For his services during this time our interpreter, Captain de Rosen, was awarded the *Croix de Guerre* by the French Government. The British decorations somehow got mislaid en route from the base.

Derniers Fugitifs à Ypres. 1915. Copyright. Antony d'Ypres. 280415.1

CHAPTER FIVE

SECOND BATTLE OF YPRES AND HOSPITAL AT LE TOUQUET

At 5 p.m. 22 April near Langemarck, in the north of the Salient, chlorine gas was used for the first time in the war by the Germans. (The cylinders of gas were in position on 8 April, but for fourteen days the wind remained in the wrong direction.) 168 tons of the gas were discharged from 4,000 cylinders over a 4 mile front in the north of the Salient towards Pilckem Ridge, against two French divisions (45th Algerian and 87th French Territorial) and a Canadian division. The Algerian troops retreated, as the clouds of greenish gas drifted forward before a gentle wind.

Men were pointing to their throats as they fled. An 8,000 yard gap resulted in the Allied defences on the north side of the Salient. The Germans, issued with crude respirators and only four miles north of Ypres, made a cautious advance of two miles and then for no apparent reason stopped.

Certainly this was a prize example during the war of a lost opportunity by the Germans. The reason seems to be that General Falkenhayn was making an experimental attack with little further intent. The fact that no reserves had been allocated to the attack supports this view. Also the German troops feared their own gas and in failing light were only too glad to dig in as soon as possible.

The BEF Second Army commander ordered a counter-attack by units of Plumer's V Corps, supported by the 1st Canadian Brigade. They were rushed into the breach in the night during a lull in the fighting. On 23 April a counter-attack was made by the Canadians and on 24 April by the British, but heavy casualties resulted from German artillery and machine-gun fire.

Due to the heavy losses without much gain General Smith-Dorrien, the Commander of the Second Army, urged the Commander of BEF, Sir John French, not to order any further attacks, and recommended withdrawal to a line three miles east of Ypres. Despite protests his request was refused resulting in Smith-Dorrien having to order more costly attacks the following morning, 25 April.

Sir John French relieved General Smith-Dorrien of his command, replacing him with General Plumer, whose first instructions from Sir J. French were to prepare the withdrawal that General Smith-Dorrien had proposed. Marshal Foch tried to persuade Sir J. French against a withdrawal and suggested an 'offensive to retake the Langemarck region at all costs'. The withdrawal of British troops by stages to three miles east of Ypres was finally sanctioned when Sir J. French learnt on 1 May that instead of receiving reinforcements, Marshal Joffre was calling for troops to be sent from Ypres to Arras for his forthcoming offensive.

The reduced Salient was one big artillery target for the Germans who shelled and gassed the Allied troops during May. On 8 May at Frezenberg Ridge the German shell-fire resulted in heavy casualties. Chlorine gas was used on 24 May at Bellewaarde Ridge. The Germans decided after this offensive to economise on shells and ceased their attacks. This marked the end of the Second Battle of Ypres.

Chlorine gas was a novel weapon and took the Allies by surprise. The soldiers had no defence against it and many were killed outright. It was counteracted initially by clasping pads soaked in urine over the face, an effective way of neutralising the chlorine. Respirators and smoke helmets were first issued to troops in June 1915. Further improvements resulted in late 1917 (see page 67) in the successful box respirator. Twenty-seven million gas masks were made and supplied to the Allied Forces.

22 APRIL 1915

The 22 April was another spring day which had passed with a little intermittent shelling until about 6 p.m. when suddenly the French 75s around Sanctuary Wood, a quarter mile to our left, commenced 'gun-fire' for all they were worth. Our artillery joined in and presently the activity spread up the line to us. We were in the foremost point of the Salient and looking backwards towards the French lines we saw a cloud of greenish vapour slowly rolling over them. It was the first gas attack of the War although at the time we did not know it. That evening we received orders to hang on at all cost, to delay any German advance, whilst the division retired to a new line through Vlamertinghe, five miles back. The gas attack against the French had been successful and there was an undefended gap nearly five miles wide in our lines. Some of the German scouts actually reached the Menin Gate, Ypres and were killed there, but fortunately no general advance took place.

That night was a nightmare. We expected an attack from either front or rear. We knew that the gas cloud had passed behind us. Exaggerated rumours of its ravages had already filtered through, but we did not know whether we were surrounded or not. A dozen times at least a sentry saw 'something' causing a feverish burst of rapid fire to break out. Nerves were on edge, for added to the fear of this new and unknown weapon, chlorine gas, which might take us unawares in the darkness, was the knowledge that in the case of an overwhelming attack, we could expect no help from the rear. We had to fight and stick it to the last man. We sweated and cursed and bit hard on our pipes. Bursts of shrapnel came over now and again. 'Whizzbangs' knocked holes in our parapet. We could spare no men to evacuate our casualties. The slightly wounded were bound up and they carried on.

23 APRIL 1915

No dawn was ever more welcome. Whatever might happen during that day, we could at least see what we were shooting.

This was to be my lucky day. Soon after dawn when we were on the parapet giving them a 'mad minute' of rifle fire, a bullet chipped my ear, grazed my neck and set fire to the woollen helmet I was wearing. The shock knocked me flat to the bottom of the trench but it was not a serious wound and I carried on. There was intense activity on our left, where the Canadians were counter-attacking in an attempt to recapture some of the trenches that the French had lost. All day we had our fair share of spasmodic shell-fire.

I found myself stone-deaf in one ear so that at about 6 p.m. when we started to send the sick and wounded away to our first-aid post I was told to go with them to have a fresh bandage put on. I fully expected to return with the stretcher-bearers, but when our Medical Officer learned that I had been wounded twelve hours before, and had not had an anti-tetanus injection, he told me that I was a fool and packed me off to the Advanced Casualty Clearing Station on the Lille road, a mile walk across open fields. I went alone and although the path was in full view of the enemy I knew he was unlikely to waste a shell on a single individual. I came to the Clearing Station, a dug-out in a railway bank, crammed with wounded waiting for the first ambulance convoy to arrive under cover of dusk. As I was waiting, a direct hit was registered on a farmstead some four hundred yards away. It was a big 42 cm shell and when the cloud of smoke cleared the whole place had disappeared. A little later the last ambulance in my convoy got a shell to itself and was destroyed. Luckily the shell was of smaller calibre or I should not be writing this.

Shell hole made by a 'Jack Johnson' near the railway station, Ypres, April 1915. Q61632. (B.C.)

24 APRIL 1915

Those ambulance drivers were brave men. They had to return through the shelling time and again, or until they were knocked out. It was a rough journey along shell-torn tracks pitted with new craters, and how the wheels and springs withstood the strain I do not know. But I must put on record that the ambulance which drove eight miles at top speed under incredibly bad conditions was a Ford, the 'Flying Bedstead' of the music hall comedians. With me were two other casualties, one a Cameron Highlander with a shattered thigh. He tossed about in delirium and when we came to the rocky bits I had to hold him on his stretcher with my full weight. The other casualty cowered in a corner crying aloud and praying in a torrent of gibberish. Poor devil, he had been badly shell-shocked.

It was dark when we skirted Ypres. The town was deserted and great fires burned there unchecked. We passed thousands of marching troops going up to fill the gaps in our lines as we made for Poperinghe. A few hours rest in the convent that housed the CCS (Casualty Clearing Station) and then by ambulance to St Omer, where a large spinning shed had been cleared of machinery to take hundreds of stretchers. There I had my anti-tetanus injection, and I felt a little easier in mind. Our MO had rather put the wind up me about the possibility of lockjaw. The Lahore Division of Indian troops had been in the fighting and on the next stretcher lay a Gurkha, a wizened monkey-faced little man. Under his pillow he had

Right: Inhabitants leaving Ypres after the bombardment of the city 18 April 1915. Q61561(B.C.)

AEYS-MOE
N. DECONINCK-DUFLOO-BOUCHE

his kukri, the razor-sharp knife from which he would not be parted. A young RAMC doctor came round and offered him money for it, only desisting when the Gurkha became angry. Later he opened his shirt and showed me a small bag, hung around his neck, containing ears – dried human ears. I have little knowledge of the Gurkha and his ways, so whether it was usual to carry around such a grisly talisman I do not know.

Then on by ambulance train to Etaples and finally at 9.30 p.m. to the Duchess of Westminster's Hospital at Le Touquet. Straight to bed inexpressibly dirty and lousy with a blood-matted beard that caused my nurse to address me as 'Dad'. I was all in.

In peace-time the Hospital had been the Casino and my bed was in the play room, an apartment of noble proportions, with all its red and gold decorations hidden under white paint. The contrast between this clean and efficient hospital and the filth I had left only a few hours before was overwhelming. I protested that I was in no fit state to sleep in a spotless bed. 'Don't be awkward, Dad' said the Sister in charge gently. I slept like a log for thirteen hours.

A nurse's uniform suited Constance, Duchess of Westminster, as indeed it suits every woman. In her bosom she wore a red cross, fashioned of rubies.

The Casino, Le Touquet, taken over for use as the 'Duchess of Westminster Military Hospital'. This photo shows the ward in which Ellison slept — once the playroom of the Casino.

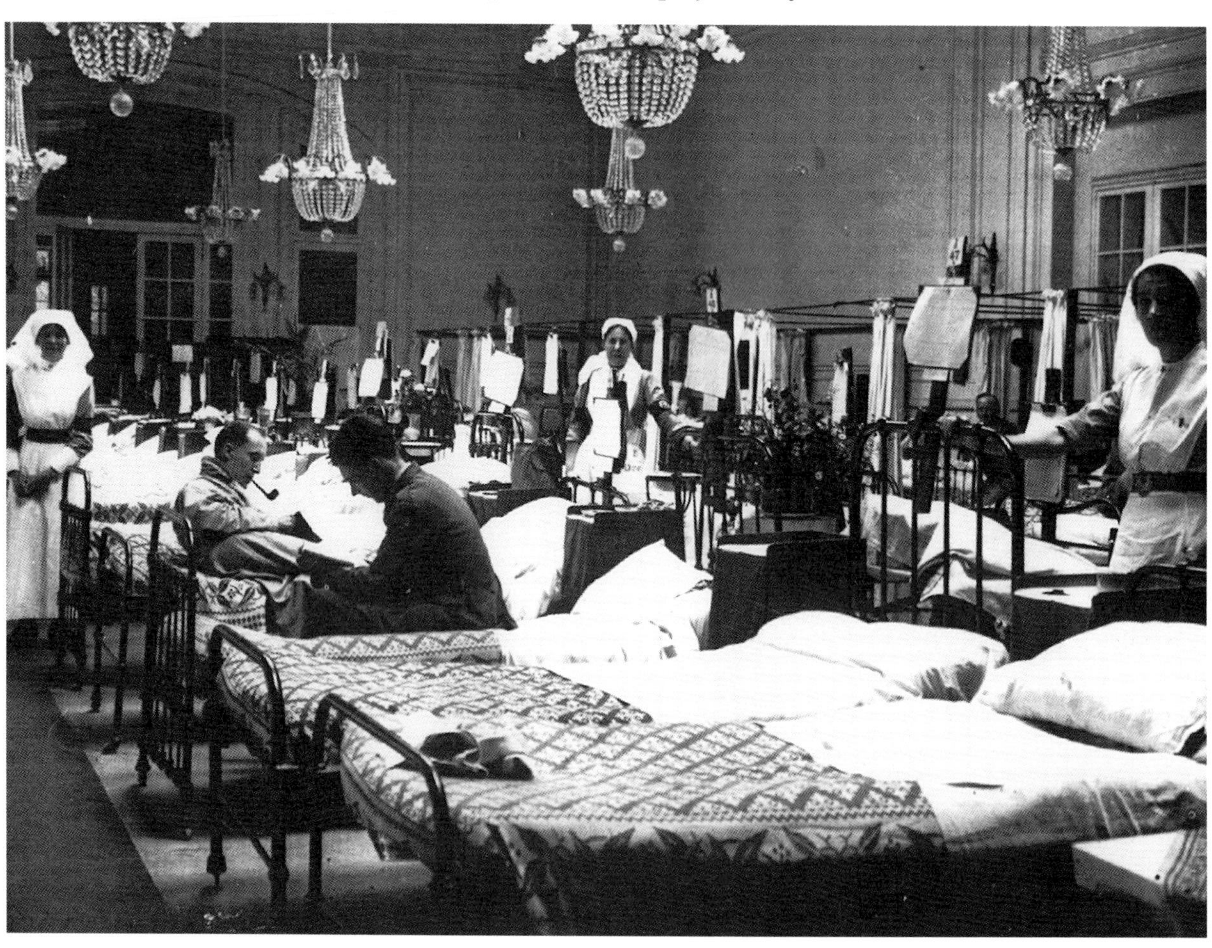

She was petite, vivacious and charming. Every morning she made a tour of the wards with cigarettes and a cheery word for each patient. Maybe it appeared a little theatrical, but I understand the Duchess paid the running costs of the hospital out of her own pocket.

The sun was warm, so that I lay on the lawn in my dressing gown and read books. I shall never forget the peace of that week in hospital.

25 APRIL 1915. LETTER FROM NORMAN ELLISON TO HIS MOTHER

Duchess of Westminster's Hospital, Le Touquet, Paris-Plage (Pas de Calais).

My dear Mother,
You will see from the above address where I am. I tried to stop a bullet with the top part of my left ear and got the worst of the encounter. This was at 4 a.m. last Friday, but I stuck at the trench until 6 p.m. that evening when I got a motor ambulance and arrived here last night after a long but comfortable train journey. It is only a slight wound and I am very glad to have it as it gives me a chance to rest. It was my thirteenth day in the trenches, the last four of which were a jolly sight too hot in the fighting to be comfortable. All this trouble over a very tiny sort of Hill too.

Don't send me any parcels here as they will not be delivered – letters are all right of course. I want you to keep a weekly paper relating to this latest fighting until I ask you to send it – it will be of particular interest to me. Any parcels which are on the way will be returned to you so keep them until I am away from here. I am quite happy and contented and getting every possible care and luxury. Write as much as possible.

Love to all,
Norman.

LETTER FROM NORMAN ELLISON'S FATHER

Frank Evans enclosed a slip of paper in a letter he wrote home and his father brought it to the office. He gives you great praise and so do all the fellows for the way you stuck to it.
I am proud to hear of it.
Good luck and best love from all,
Your affectionate father,
Fred Ellison.
Mother will write on Sunday as usual.

26 APRIL 1915

I little thought I should spend my birthday in hospital, but as it is a sight more comfortable than the trenches I am well content. Owing to bandages etc, I have not shaved for over a week and have a good half-inch beard. 'Daddy' my nurse calls me; she is very Irish and a jolly good sort. You can have no idea of the magnificence of this hospital. It was in peace times the Casino and is a large, handsome building quite close to the sea. I am in the 'play room', all its lavish gold Jewish-palace decorations have been whitened over and it is now cool and altogether delightful. The feeding here is of the best. I had a whole chicken to myself for dinner yesterday followed by milk pudding and oranges. I have also had a bath and a change of underclothing – the first for two months – so I am feeling pretty good.

Beds were needed for more serious cases so still in bandages I was whisked away to Marlborough Convalescent Camp, overlooking Boulogne from which on a clear day the white chalk cliffs of England could be seen.

One of my room mates was Nat Gubbins of the 20th City of London Territorials. He was a cub reporter on the *Daily Express* and as I am interested in writing we became friends. We could not get a bath in the camp, so one afternoon, after washing up all the cups and plates in a big zinc bath in one of the recreation huts, we persuaded the titled lady in charge, to keep guard at the door, whilst we had a good hot dip in the same zinc bath (see page 148).

When I left hospital in Le Touquet the padre gave me a pocket testament with the words 'You will be going up to the line again shortly, so good luck to you. Read this little book when you can, but always remember this – there is only one good German and that is a dead one'. He was an unctuous, over-fed, smarmy creature who had never heard a shot fired in anger and his remark sickened me. It needed all my strength to stop planting my fist in his smug face.

MARLBOROUGH CAMP. BOULOGNE DEPOT

This Rest Camp is beautifully situated on one of the hills overlooking Boulogne. It is a pleasure to see and smell the old English Channel again. I was in the CWS Hut having tea when a Belgian gentleman positively insisted on taking my photo, seated beside a fierce looking Algerian. He looked like an Arab sheik in long flowing white robes. I suppose I must look like a bit of a curio all bandaged up. I have lost all my kit and have not even a toothbrush to my name.

How charming these French villages are after filthy frowsy Flanders. We went a short walk this afternoon, the halt, the maimed and the blind. You never saw such a motley crew. We were led by a Black Watch piper. It is the first time I have marched to the bagpipes; it is rather difficult to keep step. The French are a canny people. They will not accept Belgian money, although in Belgium, French money is readily accepted.

12 MAY 1915

In due course I was marked 'Active' and sent to the Territorial Base Details Camp at Rouen, where we arrived after a trying journey in cattle trucks lasting twenty-two hours. I was pleased to see the funny cobbled winding streets of Rouen once again. The country we passed through in the train was beautiful. The foliage seemed almost tropical in its abundance and colouring, the cherry trees were all in full bloom, not a leaf to be seen but simply bough-bent with clustered clumps of blossom. I was amazed at the number and tameness of the magpies we saw bordering the line.

24 MAY 1915

I had a 'long' pass for 'Rouen' yesterday, Sunday. Whilst there I saw a number of German prisoners working on the quays (under guard of course). I must say that I have never seen such a downcast lot. Rouen is crowded with both French and English military. I think the shops must be making very comfortable little fortunes. The women here are keen on the 'Jocks' and wear all sorts of weird plaids and outlandish tartans. One girl has just passed who is pseudo-Scottish from head to toe. Even her shoe tops were a Joseph's coat of many colours. Many of these fashion plates also wear very daring imitations of military uniforms. They have little idea how absurd they make themselves. The heat here is well-nigh unbearable; it is a Turkish bath effort to light a cigarette.

30 MAY 1915

Yesterday we were down on the docks deep in the hold of a steamer shovelling coal into bags. It was extremely hot. We were rapidly turned into a mob of Gurkha-like images. On the way back to the camp we met another fatigue party who had been humping bags of flour and were as white as angels. The result was a pierrot troupe of 'Black and white artistes' and it caused considerable merriment as we marched through the town.

5 JUNE 1915

You strike funny incidents. Coming down here from Boulogne our train halted for a little while at Abbeville, so we all swarmed out of the trucks and raided a goods-train engine for hot water to make tea. The driver was a sport and it was great fun poking about its innards and hunting for weird pipes connecting with its boiler. Who said that Tommy was not ingenious? The Canadians are fine fellows and the most independent lot I have ever struck. For instance a batch went 'up the line' tonight and before they left, they were paraded before the CO for the customary speech wishing them 'Good Luck'. Now a CO's parade in the British Army is about the most solemn and formal function there is, but these boys do not care tuppence about army etiquette and formalities. On roll-call instead of the usual 'Here Sir', it is 'Sure' or 'Right here' or 'That's me'. When the CO had spoken to them they started cheering and one fellow shouted out quite loudly 'Waal – he's a b***** good scholar, anyway' in the broadest Canadian accent.

Shell bursting in Ypres. May 1915. Q61639. (B.C.)

CHAPTER SIX
ZILLEBEKE, YPRES

Ellison describes some particularly unpleasant months at Zillebeke, also referred to in a short item written for a Liverpool Rifles Reunion in the 1930s in which he recalled the discomfort of the cramped 'rat-holes' in the banks of the Lake, and the danger of the often twice-nightly journey with supplies of ammunition and mining stores to the Front line near Hill 60. Trenches were often occupied by rats and lice. Epidemics of trench fever were common. It had some of the symptoms of influenza and some of those of typhoid. It was not until 1918 that its cause was traced to an organism transmitted in the excreta of the body louse.

Both Norman Ellison and the War Correspondent Sir Philip Gibbs suffered from the disease. Gibbs was taken into the Hospital at Amiens towards the end of 1916, after the Somme battles. He was worn out after five months strain and nervous wear and tear. He writes 'I fell victim to this disease and alarmed my friends one night by giving deep sepulchral groans and calling out all sorts of nonsense in bad French and worse German. When I was carried in on a stretcher the rosy-cheeked young orderly, after taking my temperature and feeling my pulse, said "That's all right. You're going to die!" It was his way of cheering a patient up.'

17 JUNE 1915. ZILLEBEKE LAKE, NEAR YPRES

After a few days rest, the battalion returned on 12 May 1915 to the Hill 60 area to dug-outs along the steep bank of Zillebeke Lake, the reservoir that supplied Ypres. I left Rouen on the 15 June and rejoined the battalion two days later.

The battalion found that perhaps one-tenth could find accommodation in the dug-outs, yet cover from the ever threatening rain and, more important, from shell-fire was of the utmost urgency. They proceeded to dig themselves in and before nightfall, were safely tucked away in a series of shallow holes roofed with ground-sheets, sandbags, corrugated iron or whatever could be scrounged at short notice, each holding two or three men.

For nearly two months they were to remain, unrelieved in this cramped and comfortless spot, unbathed, never undressed and from Colonel downwards inexpressibly lousy. The top of the bank was under direct enemy observation from Hill 60, barely a mile distant, and during daylight our sentries kept constant watch for aeroplanes. It was amusing to see the whole battalion dive into their burrows like so many startled rabbits at the first blast of the warning whistle. At night a patrol saw that no chink of light showed from the carefully shaded candles.

20 JUNE 1915. A DUG-OUT, ZILLEBEKE LAKE

The dug-out I am in at present is cosy as dug-outs go, about 5 ft by 4 ft. It is simply a hole dug in a steep clay bank and boarded over. When three of us get in it is perhaps just a bit squashed, but that makes for warmth. Although it is June the nights are chilly enough. The large parcel ('Wardrobe for Ellison' was shouted out at the mail distribution) greeted me on my return from a particularly disagreeable forty-eight hours in the trenches and so was doubly welcome. We had some very heavy thunder and rain which soon had everything, including ourselves, covered with liquid clay. Coming back along a communication trench well

Above: Zillebeke Lake. 1916.

over our boot-tops in water, the humorist of the Company said 'Pass the word along – keep a sharp look-out for submarines.'

The flies up in the trenches are a plague, literally millions of them. You can hear them all around you like the drone of a great factory. There are also stinks (more than mere smells), which in comparison would classify Widnes as a health resort. 'Nuff said!

The other day we went to an old brewery at

Below: Zillebeke Lake near Ypres 1996.

Dickebusche, and had most enjoyable hot baths in the beer vats there.

During this period in support, our nightly duty was to supply large parties to carry ammunition and mining stores to the Front line on Hill 60. All the main fighting had moved further north to Hooge-Railway Wood area, but our own sector was far from quiet. This nightly journey – on occasions twice-nightly – was a more nerve-racking and dangerous job than holding a Front line trench. There one did have some measure of protection from fire, some hole into which one could crouch with imagined security, but this open and exposed approach up the Railway Cutting from Zillebeke Halte was a death-trap. Never a journey but the message 'stretcher-bearers' was passed down the ranks.

Only those who once formed part of that winding snake of men, over-burdened with coils of wire, corrugated iron, sleepers or balks of timber, stumbling in pitch darkness over sleepers and into shell-holes, with the leading man barely moving, yet the rear files running in a lather of sweat to keep in touch, with shells arriving punctually every few minutes at recognised danger spots and with the evil swish of machine-gun bullets overhead, can possibly appreciate the hardships we endured.

After five consecutive weeks of this very trying work, we took over a two-company frontage, between Hill 60 and Sanctuary Wood, a very difficult and exposed portion of the line. By their gas attack on the 5 May, the Germans had captured and still held all the Front line and some of the support trenches along this sector.

Since then there had been apparently neither the time nor the labour to reconstruct any trench system and now we were called upon to hold a bare line of sandbag parapet, with no support or communicating trenches and no protecting parados at the rear. Support 47 Trench was the weakest link in the chain. Half was held by us and the other half by the enemy, only a few yards separating the posts. For several hundred yards the line was held by isolated posts. If he had wished, the enemy could have walked into long empty stretches of trench any night. Theoretically the line was untenable and that we did maintain it was largely due to the accurate battery fire of the Royal Artillery. At any sign of trouble, they shelled the enemy trenches, but a few yards distance from ours. The accuracy of the shooting was remarkable; the shells seemed to skim over our heads by inches.

3 JULY 1915. A FRONT LINE TRENCH, YPRES SALIENT

I am writing this seated in a trench which has a million flies, the same number of smells and the reputation of being the nearest to Berlin. A few yards away it cuts through the ruins of a farmhouse. In fact the walls, or what remains of them, are embodied in the parapet. Just behind are the rough graves of the farmer and his wife shot by the Germans as they passed by. Why, I don't know. Today is our forty-fifth consecutive day up here – alternative spells in trenches and dug-outs. It is exceedingly hot and the mosquitoes are very troublesome. Several fellows have been badly bitten and gone into hospital.

There is fun to be had even out of this rotten game. You may remember the humorous drawings of Alfred Leete in *London Opinion* called 'The Adventures of Schmidt the Spy'? Well we threw over a copy into the Jerry lines – at this spot they are only ten yards distant, and he got frightfully annoyed and lobbed a few bombs back, without damage luckily. In this trench we have to maintain, during daylight, a 'Sausage guard' whose business it is to keep an eye open for 'Sausages' sailing through the air. I had better explain that a 'Sausage' is a cigar-shaped bomb weighing about 200 lb, discharged from a powerful Howitzer. They wobble towards you, high up in the air, like a large Rugby football. They kick up a big din when they explode. If you keep your hair on, you can dodge them, but several of the lads have run blindly into the burst – usually *'fini'*.

Drinking water is a bit of a problem here. A little way down the trench a wee burn comes trickling beneath the parapet. It looks clean decent water and is most tempting when your bottle is empty, but it flows from Jerry's lines and we are forbidden to drink it as maybe it's poisoned.

There is a fair amount of stuff flying about just now, but way above my head a skylark is singing most cheerily. Probably he has a nest and youngsters somewhere in No-Man's Land. He is getting on with his job in life anyhow, which is more than we are doing. I think his shrill pipe is one of derision for the poor d***** fools beneath him. No doubt it is a highly scientific proposition to hurl a cwt of steel five miles and blow a man to bloody fragments, but just on the moment, this cheeky little bird rather blurs my appreciation of the Triumphal Onward March of Civilisation.

Many thanks for the fine parcel just received. Socks, tea-tablets, candles and some notepaper would be welcomed in your next. Goodness alone knows when we shall see a shop again and as for a bath – I expect I shall discover that lost cardigan when I have soaked for an hour or two.

For three days in mid-July I had been on light duties with a touch of Trench fever and as my temperature would not come down I was given a lift to a Rest Station at Boeschepe in an empty motor-wagon that had brought up RE stores. We drove through Ypres, a city of the dead: not a light, not a sound, not a movement. Its only occupants a few military policemen and some engineers keeping the roads clear after the nightly shelling. We did not see a soul. The deathly silence was uncanny. A full moon threw into bolder relief the tottering walls and heaps of rubble.

Our wagon pulled up in the deep shadow of a shattered building. 'Stick by the bus, chum,' said the ASC driver, 'while me and my mate attends to some orders. Shan't be too long.' They vanished into the shadows and left me with my thoughts and a head buzzing like a saw-mill. Presently they returned with their 'orders', a sewing machine and two bicycles looted from some abandoned house. I was glad when we were well clear of Ypres as looting is a serious army crime and I did not want to be mixed up in any trouble of that kind.

The next day my temperature was still too high so I was sent for a rest to the Mont-des-Cats Monastery, which the RAMC had turned into an Advanced Hospital.

19 JULY 1915. NO 3 WARD, RAMC, MONT-DES-CATS MONASTERY

I have written letters to you from some queer spots but never before from a monk's cell. This cubicle – there are about eighty of them in this dormitory – is dedicated to Saintus Augustinus. A lettered board over the doorway informs me that the previous occupant was one Frère Alphonsus.

This monastery is a wonderful place, the buildings are comparatively modern and cover a large area. It is a farm on a big scale, with all sorts of crops, cattle, pigs and a very large kitchen garden with splendid fruit trees, especially the pears and peaches. They make their own cheese, butter and wine and seem to be a self-contained community. A number of the monks are still here. I imagine they belong to some very strict order as they do not speak to each other, but use signs. They dress in the roughest of serge. You cannot imagine how peculiar it seems to see these people doing all sorts of odd jobs, harnessing horses etc, in their medieval rig-out. We are still, however, within sound of the guns.

One of the oddest sights I have seen out here is a very large sow which had both its ears blown off when the monastery was shelled last November. I fed it with scraps of bread and cannot help laughing every time I see it.

In early August 1915, we left Zillebeke and the Salient for, we hoped, a very long time. I rejoined the battalion at Abeele the day before they left.

CHAPTER SEVEN

THE PEACEFUL SOMME

Norman Ellison's battalion was posted from Flanders to the Somme region in August 1915, almost a year before the Somme Battles commenced on 1 July 1916. The countryside was green and still fairly unspoilt. He was billeted for a time in Meaulte on the southern outskirts of Albert. He mentions the famous gilded statue of the 'leaning Virgin' on top of the basilique of Notre-Dame-des-Brebieres. Situated on the River Ancre, which joins the Somme at Corbie, Albert was until the early seventeenth century known as Ancre. A major British administrative and control centre for the Somme offensive of July 1916, it was captured by the Germans in March 1918 but recaptured by the British during the Battle of Amiens in August 1918. The town was rebuilt in the 1920s in the art deco style, the basilique being rebuilt to its original design.

The Tunnelling Companies were active in the trenches facing Fricourt during August 1915. Ellison describes having the unpleasant and difficult job of assisting the tunnellers by removing excavated debris in narrow tunnels twenty feet underground. In October 1915, south of Albert near the Somme river, Ellison describes a meeting with the War Correspondent Sir Philip Gibbs in Vaux Woods. A strange kind of truce existed between the Allies in the village of Vaux and the Germans in the village of Curlu. Gibbs writes in his autobiography:*

'The village of Curlu was actually beyond our Front line, and was a kind of outpost in No-Man's Land, within five hundred yards or so of another village held by the Germans in advance of their own Front line. Between these two villages was a thicket of silver birches and willows, half of which belonged to us and half to the enemy. By tacit understanding on both sides neither of these villages was shelled.

Our officers – they were Loyal North Lancashires – used to go to bed every night in their pyjamas. I had a meal with them there, and they told me of this strange truce inherited from the French. They were all for it. One of them took me into the thicket, telling me not to speak or cough. Stealing through the trees, we came on two men dressed in green, with green veils over their faces, and green gloves. Beyond them if we had walked a few yards we should have bumped into German sentries. Occasionally there was an exchange of shots in the thicket, and sometimes a real fight, but as a rule there was peace and as a token of pax each side retired behind a wicker gate which was then shut. From the Front line behind I looked into both villages and saw German soldiers moving about in theirs and – fantastically strange! – a woman wheeling a perambulator.

This state of things lasted until the Battles of the Somme when both villages were blown off the map.'

The Vaux area of the Somme described by Ellison with its lagoons, marshes, and aspen trees remains a beautiful area, but eighty years later the British, French and German troops have been replaced by tourists and weekend anglers. During September and until the end of November the trapping of mature silver eels – commencing their journey back to their breeding ground in the Sargasso Sea – takes place at several trapping stations known as anguilleres.

* Ref Ch 7. *'War Underground. The Tunnellers of the Great War'* by Alexander Barrie.

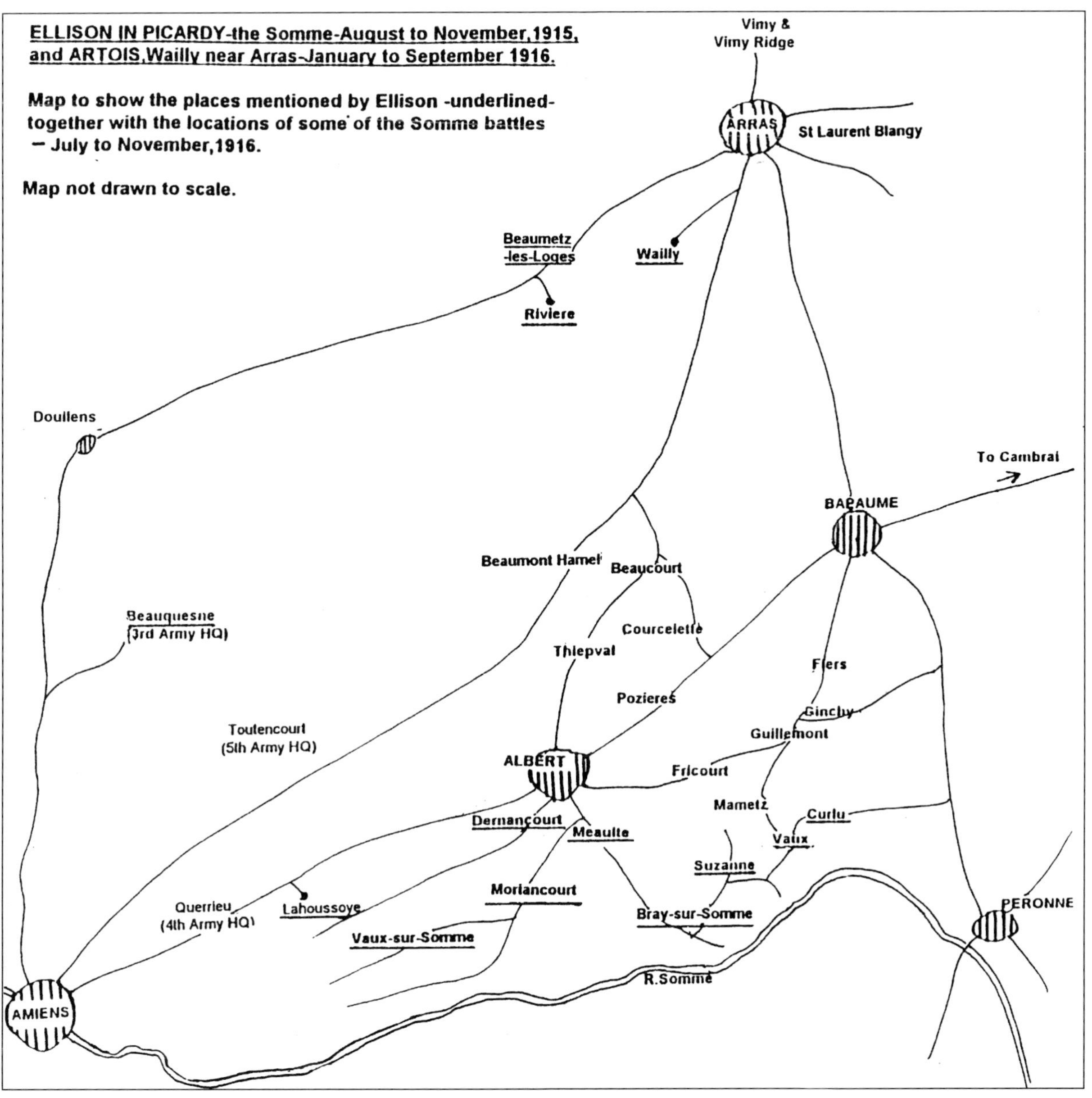

1 AUGUST 1915

We left the desolation of Flanders behind and went south to rural France proper. It was a very different terrain of long rolling down, of scruffy turf with the underlying white chalk breaking through in places; a well wooded countryside that looked intensely fresh and green. We were the first British troops there, and so the natives and their houses, the food and wine had not yet become Anglicised.

The village we are in now, La Houssoye, was in the occupation of the Germans for a fortnight during September last. Also during the 1870 war they were through it. Last night I was talking to an old dame who had remained in the village during both occupations. She had some interesting tales to tell me. On the door of her small cottage was painted: '*EPICERIE' Madame Veuve Bochet, devouée pour la patrie, ce qui fait qu'on l'appelle La Maman des Soldats.*

15 AUGUST 1915. A HAY-LOFT, MEAULTE

Beer is also a luxury we have not yet discovered since arriving in rural France proper. Nothing to drink but red wine, fearful stuff at best. As I write there is a very heavy thunderstorm bursting overhead, but the sound of Nature's artillery seems very weak and feeble compared with ours below.

The other day I was one of a guard at a cross-roads some little distance outside this place. Our job was to find out the business of everyone who passed. Our guard room was a deserted inn which the inhabitants had evidently left hurriedly when it was shelled. We explored the place thoroughly and found plenty of crockery, glassware, saucepans etc, so we set about making a good meal. Also I would just mention that there was a kitchen garden, fruit trees and a large pigeon-loft. Here is our menu for the day:

Breakfast. Bacon and fried pigeon's eggs, jam, bread and butter, tea and coffee.

Dinner. Boiled meat, a stew of two pigeons, carrots, onions, beans and potatoes.

Tea. Stewed prunes, stewed rhubarb and stewed greengages, spring onions and lettuce, bread and butter and tea.

Supper. Six boiled pigeons.

I don't think you can beat that for a good day's foraging.

The country round here is a cross between the Yorkshire moors and the South Downs. There is a complete absence of trees and shrubs which makes it good fighting ground. The soil is poor and the limestone comes within two feet of the surface practically everywhere. As a result it is quite impossible to hide trenches from the enemy as the excavated material looks like a long white snake winding across the countryside. There are a great number of kestrels and sparrowhawks about here. Whilst on guard recently I counted thirty-one kestrels hovering over a large field of corn-stubble, all at the same time. Of course everywhere is swarming with rats and mice.

From our billets in Meaulte we saw for the first time the famous 'leaning Virgin' of Albert. From the dome of the cathedral tower, this gilt statue, struck by a chance shell, hung outwards horizontally and held that position apparently by a miracle. It was widely believed in France that the army which held Albert when the statue fell, would lose the war. By coincidence, the Virgin was brought down by gunfire during the German occupation of the town in the spring of 1918.

We were soon in the trenches again facing Fricourt. Real trenches this time carved out of the solid chalk rock and often ten to twelve feet in depth. Here there fell to our lot the most unpleasant of tasks – acting as labourers to the miners down the saps. To crawl on hands and knees along a narrow tunnel twenty feet underground, choked with thick chalk dust and blinded with sweat, dragging a sandbag filled with the excavated debris from the working face to the windlass rope at the foot of the entrance shaft, with air becoming so foul, that presently the candles would flicker and die out. It was no easy job. Add to this a feeling of oppression, of being caged in, intensified by the perceptible earth tremors from the heavy shells and trench mortars bursting on the surface above, and the sure knowledge that the enemy was countermining – could we not hear faintly their pick strokes in the half hours of 'listening' between our labours?

It was largely a matter of luck which side 'blew' the other's gallery first, and it will be appreciated why we detested the work. Of bravery in the face of fire, no one unit in the Army had the monopoly, yet for downright consistent heroism, the underground work of the Tunnelling Companies, composed for the most part of coal-miners, could not be equalled.

26 AUGUST 1915. A BARN, MORLANCOURT

This morning we have all been through a gas 'attack', that is to say we all went into a closed room wearing our respirators and the gas was turned on. You taste it slightly; the respirators are splendid things.

On 1 September 1915 we marched to Suzanne and relieved the 5th Cheshires in one of the most interesting sectors of the line. The usual defence system of trenches could not be used there as the broad volume of the River Somme took a great horseshoe bend and enclosed an area, roughly oval in shape and perhaps a mile across, formed of marshes, pools and channels, with occasional well-wooded 'islands'. On either side of the oval rose high land. We held one height, the enemy the other. Across this waterlogged 'No-Man's Land', wandered a narrow footpath or two, but anything in the nature of a frontal attack in force was impossible. Fighting patrols were sent out from both sides and kept the ground neutral. From our cliff-top we could look down into the enemy village of Curlu. They overlooked our village of Vaux, so there came into being a tacit understanding 'to live and let live' and neither place was shelled.

A small bridge crossing the sluice-gates at the end of the village of Vaux led to a rough track – the Causeway – which disappeared into the high reeds and osiers of the marshes. After some 300 yards it ended in a sandbagged 'block'. A further 400 yards deeper into the marshes was established the Duck Post, a substantial sandbagged strong-point held by some twenty men. In front of it was a rough semicircle of isolated sentries hidden in the scrub woodland. Between the watchers, trip wires were hidden, whilst the only path an advancing enemy could take between the water on either side, was guarded by a hollow 'drum-bridge' upon which the lightest footfall was audible. Each side laid carefully prepared ambushes for the other. Patrols met and fought it out. Several medals for bravery were won by our scouts. My friend Jimmy Rivers took part in one of these encounters and yarning together one night a few years later I wrote this down at his dictation:

> 'We had just got to the edge of the Third Wood when Wilson who was acting "point", saw a face in the bushes. He gave the alarm and we all fell flat just as Jerry opened fire. Young Parry was not quick enough and was killed. We actually could not see anybody, but we had a good idea where the shots were coming from and we replied heavily. One of the Germans got up and commenced to run back, maybe for reinforcements, but we riddled him. You could not miss at fifty yards range. After the first shot my rifle jammed so I crawled over to Parry who had been killed and got his.
>
> The sudden burst of fire in such a quiet part of the line attracted one of our aeroplanes and it came swooping low down to discover the trouble. Afterwards we heard that he had reported great "wind-up" in Curlu – loading limbers and carts preparatory to quitting. Jerry must have thought that we were attacking in force. We continued blazing away for nearly an hour but gradually the German fire became less and finally died away. By this time more of our fellows had come up from Vaux and it was decided to clear the wood. We charged but they had gone. Rifles, helmets and equipment lay scattered about but they had cleared away their casualties. Great pools and tracks of blood and a field dressing covered with brains showed that they had suffered considerably.
>
> Listening post on the marshes was always a nervy job but after this scrap it became doubly so. The most advanced sentry would be about forty yards ahead of the "Duck Post". There you lay hidden in the bushes absolutely alone, motionless and silent for two hours, with every sense on edge for the least sound. You knew that there was nothing between you and the German lines, unless some of our scouts were

out, and that probably in the undergrowth about you their scouts were prowling around. You had an uncanny feeling that unseen eyes were watching and waiting patiently for you to become a good target. The most commonplace things happening – the drip of rain on fallen leaves, the scurrying of rats or water-fowl – became magnified into an invisible enemy attacking your hiding place. Vaux itself was a "cushy" place but out on the marshes was a continued strain. No wonder some of the fellows "saw things", and raised false alarms.'

The Germans never got over the rout of their carefully prepared ambush within two hundred yards of their own village and, during the further month the battalion held this sector, they did not send out another patrol. The mastery of the marshes had definitely passed into our keeping.

Our scouts had learnt much from a Captain and section of Pathan Scouts from the Indian Army, who had been attached to us for a while. The work they had been engaged upon was a closely guarded secret, but as they were frequently through and well behind the enemy lines, there is little doubt it was connected with the collection of reports from our Secret Service agents stationed in occupied territory. These Pathans were masters of scoutcraft. Dressed in overalls, camouflaged with yellow and green paint splashes, with faces and hands likewise disguised and an upstanding fringe of rushes as headgear, they became part of the undergrowth, through which they could creep without snapping a twig. Had their orders been to fight, they could have wiped out the enemy patrols with ease, for sometimes as one of our scouts was creeping along with elaborate caution, his ankle would be seized by a hand, and looking down in alarm he would see the laughing face of a Pathan silently enjoying the success of his little joke.

In the meantime, the rest of the battalion lived in comparative comfort. A little digging, road mending and dug-out building under a minimum of shell-fire was a welcome contrast to the terrible 'fatigues' we had been used to up north. In the woods we became experts at weaving withies into fascines and camouflage screens. The river abounded in fish and in peaceful days had supplied eels to the Paris market. All sorts of improvised fishing tackle appeared, whilst those lacking the true patience of your true angler frequently added to their rations by bombing the river. Ducks, in a semi-wild state, did not appear on the menu until an ingenious mind baited a spring rat-trap and floated it down amongst them on a board fastened to a line. This was easy 'fishing', for no duck could resist such an easy meal.

9 SEPTEMBER 1915. A DUG-OUT, VAUX-SUR SOMME

We are in a wood and all the avenues and paths are named with signboards on the plan roughly of Chester – Watergate Street, Bridge Street etc. Last night I was on outpost duty and distinctly heard a German band playing and singing behind their lines. This war is one huge paradox and although I have been out here seven months now, rarely a day passes but something strikes me as being out of place and absurd amid the horrors and general hellishness inseparable from a conflict of this size.

It is a common saying out here that Fritz spends more money bombarding a town than it cost to build originally, and I quite believe it. You have little idea of the stuff they 'plonk' into a place once they start and I should say that a great deal is of really no value from a military point of view.

11 SEPTEMBER 1915

Re Commission. I am not at all surprised at the delay with the War Office. Kitchener has not managed to abolish all the red tape yet. The weather during the daytime is simply sweltering, but at night it becomes bitterly cold; indeed it is quite a problem to keep warm as it is really too early for blankets to be served out. We went through some hellish hardships when we first came out, and some little appreciation of the comfortable life we had given up of our own free-will, was, I think, due to us. I feel very strongly on this point and shall not forget it. Since I came out here I have learnt to judge men by what they are – not by what they profess to be.

The mosquitoes ('skeeters') here are persistent devils; they positively thrive on anti-fly creams and such things. Our faces are swollen with bites. We can scarcely recognise each other.

Just at present we are working every minute of the day building and improving dug-outs for winter quarters. We are on one side of a steep valley with the Germans on the other. In between stretch marshes and creeks making trenches there an impossibility, so both sides have to fall back on patrol and outpost work. This is more like the genuine article, fighting in open country. It is a welcome change from trench life where you are penned in your so many given yards of ground. When we get things a bit ship-shape I hope to have a little fishing in the river. I understand there is fine sport to be had. It is an absolute necessity that I should keep my kit to the rock-bottom minimum. In this particular little patch of country the lanes are already ankle deep in mud and slush, so winter here will not be a picnic.

17 SEPTEMBER 1915. A BARN, SUZANNE

Fruit is very plentiful, especially apples and in a little while the walnuts will be ripe for eating.

The first signs of autumn are to hand. The swallows are congregating for their journey south and many of the trees have commenced to shed their leaves.

On this game one becomes used to all sorts of queer jobs. The other day we all went for a hot bath, and welcome it was too. I had the job of hot-ironing the tunics. Rather an interesting business chasing 'big game' with a hot flat iron.

Suzanne was the usual untidy French village of a single street running down a steep hill to the empty Château at the bottom. The road at the top was under enemy observation and along it, the owner of the Château and a girl on a white horse used to take occasional rides and by some pre-arranged signs thus indicate the positions of gun batteries. Both were shot as spies by the French, then occupying this part of the line. Whether it was rumour or fact I never discovered.

I was lucky: my Company was posted to Vaux Wood where we occupied dug-outs, each holding about a dozen men. They had been constructed originally by the French and we had the luxury of wire-netting beds. The biggest curse were rats. More than once I have been awakened by one snuggling into my blankets for warmth, when I would roll over on my back and smother it.

17 OCTOBER 1915. A DUG-OUT, VAUX WOOD

The rats here swarm everywhere in thousands. Nothing is safe from them. Suspend the food in a sandbag from the roof and as soon as you are asleep they swarm down the string and get at it. At dusk we chase and strafe them with sticks. I had the record bag the other night, twenty-three inches from nose to tip of tail, as big as a rabbit. When you are bedded down they run all over you, so you get your face under the blanket. Unwholesome brutes.

These beds are alarming affairs of wire-netting stretched over a sort of rustic wooden framework. They are comfortable enough when you get to know the hang of them. Although not so warm as straw, they are free from lice, and that is more than a boon and a blessing. The paths in the wood are all named after the streets in Chester, so you can guess the regiment here before us. We have done the same with the village below us here. The officers you will find billeted in the 'Angel' and they look out upon a very doubtful Exchange Flags. Then there is

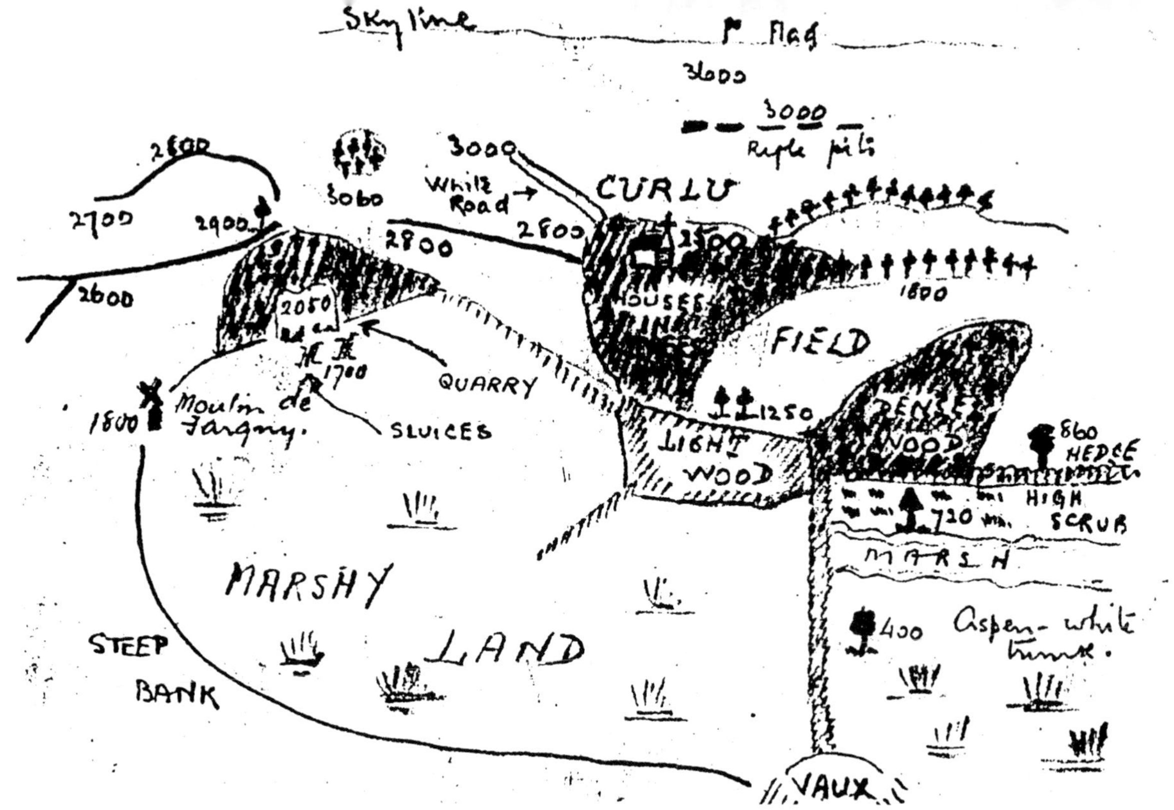

Copy of range map, from look out-post above Vaux village, shown to Sir P. Gibbs. October 1915.

Dale Street leading to Abercromby Square and a manure heap which would make the original blush. There was a bit of a blaze in a billet the other day, but we rushed out the ancient manual fire-engine still intact in the village and put it out. I think everybody enjoyed the fun. Snow has fallen heavily and the whole place is deep in slush.

12 NOVEMBER 1915. A DUG-OUT IN A WOOD, VAUX

We heard the Zeppelins returning homewards from their last murderous trip. The weather is still very wet and cold but we generally get a good fire going in the 'dug-out' at night and so manage to dry ourselves a little. I understand that we are shortly to be issued with gumboots so that at least will keep our feet dry. It is a funny thing but although our feet are often sopping wet for days on end, we do not feel any ill effects such as colds etc, only the discomfort of the feet being clammy and cold. It just shows how hardened we have become. We have been in this dug-out now for eight consecutive weeks and it would be rather interesting to see a civilian face – such as they are.

From the wood a communication trench zigzagged down the very steep side of the hill to the village. At the top was an observation post, with a sentry whose duty it was during daylight to keep watch on the German lines and more particularly on the marshes. Any suspicious sign, such as the sudden rising of waterfowl in alarm, which might give away the position of an enemy reconnoitring patrol, had to be reported immediately. One day I was on duty when an officer wearing the brassard and green cap-band of a war correspondent was brought to my post by the Officer in charge of a French artillery battery stationed in the wood. It was (Sir) Philip Gibbs, the famous war correspondent whose vivid dispatches from the Front earned him a Knighthood. Every war correspondent had a pass that enabled him to go to any part of the Front at any time, and obtain the facts or points from every class and rank from the trenches to GHQ. He asked me many questions

View from Vaux Belvedere looking towards Curlu. Recent photo by Editor. 1996.

Photo of Sir P. Gibbs (right) watching an aerial combat. September 1916. Q1062.

and through the binoculars I showed him the special points we kept under constant view. A quiet 'matey' sort of man with great charm, I took to him at once and had I known as we talked whom he was, then certainly I would have thanked him for his autobiographical novel *The Street of Adventure.* He had risen from cub reporter the hard way. I remembered his account of working on a Bolton paper for a mere pittance. He was a young married man and they had lived in a tumbledown, leaky cottage for a weekly rental of ninepence. If it rained they went to bed, baby and all, sheltered under an umbrella. As I had always wanted to enter journalism it was a great thrill to meet in person such an eminent member of the profession. He left me to go down the hillside trench into Vaux. A few days later, his dispatch in the *Daily Post*, under the heading 'Gentlemanly Ways of Warfare', described *inter alia* our meeting and what we had seen together (see pages 102–104).

Towards the end of 1915 many battalions of the new 'Kitchener's Army', as it was popularly called, had been formed. We learnt that Officer's Commissions were being granted to inexperienced youths almost straight from school, whereas men at the Front, eminently more suitable because of their experience, found every approach to HM Commission blocked. It seemed grossly unfair at the time and we said hard and bitter things about the nebulous 'they' who ordered our lives from London. My father thought he might be able to pull some strings at his end, so, as the first move in the game, I approached my Commanding Officer, Captain Westby. He agreed that I should have a commission and wrote out a chit of recommendation.

I wanted a commission if possible in the artillery. I was tired of 'foot slogging'. Possibly that was the reason why the strings my father pulled were not the right ones. Months passed and nothing happened so that eventually I abandoned the idea.

Some years later I read Field Marshal Earl French's book of memoirs, *1914,* and came to understand the attitude of the War Office. The Field Marshal wrote:

> 'I wonder sometimes if the eyes of the country will ever be opened to what these Territorial soldiers of ours have done. I say without the faintest hesitation that without the assistance which the Territorials afforded in October 1914 and June 1915, it would have been impossible to have held the line between France and Belgium, or to have prevented the enemy from reaching his goal, the Channel seaboard.'

So the first lines of our Territorial Regiments were sacrificed through the exigencies of war. Let us not blame anybody; they volunteered for a nasty job and did it.

CHAPTER EIGHT

WITH THE THIRD ARMY – BEAUQUESNE

On the 18 July 1915 a new British Army – the Third – was formed under the command of Field Marshal Allenby. By early August four divisions had taken over a seventeen mile sector to the north of the River Somme. Attached to Third Army H.Q. in November 1915, Ellison enjoyed the experience of making a daily coal round to several châteaux in the area of Beauquesne, including one occupied by Field Marshal Allenby.

He went home on his first leave on 16 December, arriving back on the 26 December. He learnt in early January of his mother's death. This altered his outlook on the war and although he had been recommended for a commission he decided not to pursue the matter. He saw coming back alive as his main priority.

Official statistics show that for the British Army, and especially the infantry, the Western Front was particularly dangerous. For every nine men sent out, five were killed, wounded or missing. An officer stood a one in six chance of being killed and a one in three chance of being wounded, and, as Ellison was aware, nearly twice as likely to be killed as another rank.

In the middle of November 1915, we were attached to Third Army HQ at Beauquesne as Army troops with a wide variety of duties – guards, traffic control, typists, clerks, telephone operators, grooms. In fact there was no job we did not tackle. Thus it came about that a joiner and a bank clerk in civilian life became transformed into cobblers. With hammer and chisel and saw, they worked their will cheerfully, if not scientifically, on the men's boots until one day there came along a Staff Officer's riding boot to be stitched. Neither had the faintest idea how a boot should be sewn but they had a shot at it. I will not repeat what the Staff Officer said nor do I think it necessary to explain why our cobblers found themselves on guard duties again!

It was my good fortune to be allocated the best job of all – Coalman to the Third Army. 'They want two coalmen,' said my platoon sergeant, coming into the billet. 'You two, Ellison and Roberts, you're a pair of black beggars and the coal dust won't show on you. What about it?' We jumped at it; not only were we, more or less, our own masters, but we escaped the 'spit and polish' which permeated the whole place. An open dump of some forty tons of coal was in our care. We filled fifty-odd bags every morning and delivered them by motor lorry to various châteaux and messes on a seventeen-mile round. Snow fell on most days and so it became a dirty, slushy job, but it had ample compensations. At most of the larger châteaux there was usually a glass of wine for us; we had free entry to a 'blind tiger' – an estaminet kept open during prohibited hours by the – well, never mind, I will not give them away. A great pot of warm milk liberally laced with rum could be found there simmering on the stove throughout the day, and I know no better warming beverage when you are half frozen. You can feel the fire flowing through your veins to the very tips of your fingers and toes. One day I was leaving the château where Field Marshal Allenby lived, after humping several bags of very wet coal, when I met the great man himself strolling along a path with one of his aides. He looked at me and involuntarily exclaimed 'Good God, what?' when his aide whispered something that caused him to burst into laughter. I kept a straight face and gave him a very stiff and formal salute as he passed. This was my first personal meeting with a Field Marshal. Thirty years later I came to know one well enough to realise that they really are human beings.

19 NOVEMBER 1915 BEAUQUESNE

The cold weather still continues. The countryside is deep in snow and we have a hard frost every night. This morning I broke the ice on the rain-tub before I shaved and washed outside. Fifteen of us are billeted in a fair-sized room in an empty cottage and we are as merry and light-hearted as sheep in clover.

This town literally flows with Bass's Pale Ale and Extra Stout. You cannot possibly imagine how we appreciate a pipe and a glass in a snug corner of an estaminet. It is only then that we think of the rough patches we struck 'up there'.

I suppose you have read how motor-drivers out here have a habit of naming their lorries – such as *Flying Dutchman, Sister Susie, Lumbering Luke* and so on. I saw one the other day called *Marley's Ghost* and it struck me as being a particularly appropriate name for a several ton accumulation of clinking and clanging metal.

I still go on my daily coal-round and really enjoy it, as we go right out into the country to serve several châteaux. The countryside is really beautiful just at present. The warm autumnal tints have sobered down to the cold green and olives which dominate so many of Constable's pictures. This is an open country of rolling hills and winding valleys very similar to our own Downs

We have now got our mess in working order (fifteen of us), and very snug and comfortable we are. Whittle and I do the cooking and we live like fighting cocks. Every morning we open the ball with porridge, bacon and fried bread, honey or jam and tea. Luncheon mid-day: steak and onions or mutton chops. Dinner 6.30 p.m.: soup, roast beef or mutton, potatoes and another vegetable, milk pudding and jam, cake, coffee and cigarettes. There just remains time to go out and have a glass of Bass, 'pell-ell' as the natives call it, and Voila!

In England the village inns are very proud of their signboards. Here the estaminets boast very curious and often artistic weather cocks.

As I write one of the REs is playing the piano delightfully. His music is the same as Dad generally plays on a Sunday. Although I cannot remember the names of the compositions the tunes are familiar.

16 DECEMBER 1915

On 16 December 1915 I left Beauquesne on my first leave. Ten crowded days at home. I cannot describe the joy of being with my own folks again, yet, somehow, I felt myself a foreigner in a strange land. The people in Britain had not the least idea of what war really meant. Many families had lost fathers and sons and suffered the bitter poignancy of their loss, but even then they knew nothing whatsoever of the circumstances in which they had died or the conditions under which they had lived. There was a vast gulf between the civilians and the Front line soldier that no words could ever bridge. I dined with several elderly businessmen who had sons in the services. They complained of irksome war-time restrictions, of shortages of this and that, of rising prices and many other things that, seen against the background of real war, did not matter a damn. They had lost their sense of proportion. Their perspective was out of focus.

I remember one man who had made a lot of money since the war started, telling me that he could not obtain enough butter, so he had bought a farm where, he boasted, he could now get all the butter and cream he wanted. Another informed me that he had paid eight hundred pounds income tax in the previous year and had bought his wife a new sealskin coat costing one hundred and twenty guineas.

At that time these were big sums of money. I did not envy them their wealth, but I could not commend their good taste in flaunting it before a member of the PBI (Poor Bloody Infantry), who was returning 'over there' in a few days' time to face very alfresco meals and an uninsurable future.

I had to report back on the morning of Boxing Day and that meant travelling all Christmas Day. I was sorely tempted to overstay my leave, but I had a clean conduct sheet and I meant to keep it so. As events turned out, it was a wise decision.

The passage across the Channel was exceedingly rough: a stiff SW breeze and frequent rain squalls. I am glad to say that I proved a good sailor and slept soundly through the whole business. However, the rest of my party had a very bad time.

The train journey through France to Beauquesne was – as we expected – rotten in every sense. The very comprehensive curse that the Lord High Cardinal of Rheims placed on the jackdaw was a mere nothing to the week-long pent-up energy we wasted on the French State Railways.

The slow, monotonous journey was made tolerable by a bottle of rum and another of whisky that somehow came into our compartment. At Amiens station we stopped for an hour for refreshments, and there we suggested to an Army Service Corps Sergeant in the carriage that the live duck he had brought with him in a bass-bag for his Mess ought to have a swim. Just outside the station was a large water storage tank supported on a tall steel framework. The Sergeant with a good ration of rum inside him agreed. So he climbed the ladder to the top of the tank and allowed the duck to swim around. But it was a wise bird with no wish to be the 'burnt offering' at a Sergeants' Mess Dinner, so it refused to return to the angry Sergeant. 'All aboard' was sounded and the Sergeant had to scramble down the ladder empty-handed. For all that I know to the contrary, that duck may still be swimming around the tank at Amiens.

MID-JANUARY 1916

On 12 January 1916, my mother died suddenly. She was only forty-eight.

Devon Villa,
Crescent Rd,
Liscard,
Cheshire.
12 January '16.

My dear Norman,
I have the worst of news for you. Your dearest mother is dead. She had a severe stroke early on yesterday morning and never regained consciousness and passed away early this morning. The doctor is inexpressibly shocked as are all the others. This is the first blow you have had to bear in a world of grief and sorrow as well as pleasure, but you are now a man and will stand the blow fairly. I lost my father at your age.

You will remember your dear mother as one of the best, cheerful and of good advice.

I have lost my prop and mainstay.

Do not be downhearted, you have still your King and Country to fight for and when the war is over and you return we will go on with our lives in the way your mother and I were planning out.

Man proposes. God disposes. Tell your chums and they will share your grief. I expect we shall bury mother at Rake Lane cemetery on Saturday next.

With our united best love,
Your affectionate father,
Fred Ellison.

Your letter of 7th reached here on 10th. Dott and Win are bearing up very well and bravely.

I obtained compassionate leave and arrived home four days later. This unexpected blow completely altered my outlook on the war. I found my father seriously ill and unknown to anyone went to see his doctor. 'I'll try to keep him alive until you return,' he said. He did not succeed and so it seemed to me that my most important duty was to come back alive. Hitherto I had not given much thought to my family. Now it appeared likely that I might have the responsibility of two younger sisters thrust upon me. In those days the average life of a second lieutenant on active service was so short, I gave up all idea of a commission. On my return from leave I had an interview with my Company officer and CSM Tanner and put the whole case before them. They agreed to find a job for me out of the line, if at all possible. Six months later when the Battle of the Somme started both kept their word, and so, although always on the fringe of it, I missed participation in that 'blood bath', as the Germans so rightly called it.

Colour sketch by Ellison of RSM Clem Tanner. Dated 22 April 1916 – dedicatee.

Clem Tanner – An unflattering caricature of the best soldier I ever met. We started together in the same tent at Knowsley in August 1914, and there was born a friendship which I value to this day. He was then a corporal in charge of us rookies; an old volunter re-enlisted who knew all the ropes. In action, he was a very brave man with a devotion to duty outstanding in a Battalion which prided itself upon it. He rose to be acting-R.S.M., was badly wounded at Guillemont, and was awarded the Military Medal – a totally inadequate reward for what he did.

CHAPTER NINE

WAILLY, A VILLAGE NEAR ARRAS

Arras was the most important French town to be held by the British throughout the War. Norman Ellison arrived in Wailly immediately behind the Arras Front line in January 1916. The village, including the church, had been badly damaged and the inhabitants had fled. He spent some weeks in filthy trenches during very cold weather and describes how, whilst on sentry duty one night, he had a strange 'Out of Body' experience. From April to June, Wailly appears to have been comparatively quiet. He writes about the wildlife of the area and even finds time for sketching and laying out a six hole putting course!

Ellison's battalion left the Arras area at the end of July. Three months later in October 1916 the British troops in Arras constantly shelled by the Germans, decided to move underground. Beneath Arras are the famous caves used for storing wine – 'boves' – together with a network of galleries dating back to the tenth century, cut into the limestone on which the town stands.

In October 1916 the New Zealand Tunnelling Company aided by a Leeds Bantam Battalion, the 17th West Yorks, commenced work on linking the large caves and cellars beneath the centre of Arras with tunnels they drove out east and south-east of Arras.

Together with existing caves and converted sewers they provided shelter, and underground barracks, for 11,500 troops during the winter of 1916–1917. Completed by April 1917, and a unique engineering achievement, the tunnels enabled troops to be concealed and moved in safety towards the Front line. It was possible, for example, to travel underground from the centre of Arras to just behind the line at St Laurent Blangy on the east side of Arras. The caves and eight-mile maze of subways when completed were provided with running water, gas-proof doors, kitchens, sleeping quarters, ammunition dumps and a hospital. A tramline ran from the Crinchon sewer to the St Sauveur caves.*

Visitors to the Canadian Memorial Park at Vimy Ridge, north of Arras are able to take a conducted tour of part of the Grange tunnel system – not connected to those at Arras – built by the Tunnelling Companies prior to the Battle of Vimy Ridge. Part of an extensive system from the western slope of the Ridge to the Front line, the tunnels allowed troops to reach the Canadian lines in safety.

The Battles of Arras and Vimy Ridge took place in April 1917. In early December 1996 a British Army war grave containing the remains of 25 soldiers serving with the 13th Battalion Royal Fusiliers was discovered near the village of Monchy-le-Preux. Monchy saw some of the fiercest and most bloody action of the Battle of Arras in April 1917. The Battle of Arras had the highest daily rate of casualities – 4,076 – compared to the other major offensive battles fought by the British in the First World War (i.e. the Somme, Passchendaele and the Final Offensive).

* Ref Ch2 *Cheerful Sacrifice. The Battle of Arras 1917* by Jonathan Nicholls.

The Battle of the Somme commenced on 1 July 1916. Ellison moved south to Bray in the Somme region on 20 July 1916. He admits his good luck in being given a job in the transport lines when the battalion went into action. A broad chalk ridge north of the River Somme is intersected by a straight Roman road linking Albert with Bapaume. The villages of the ridge e.g. Beaumont-Hamel, Thiepval, Pozieres, Fricourt and Mametz are part of military history.

Wailly Church and Wailly Orchard Cemetry in October, 1996. Photo by editor.

JANUARY AND FEBRUARY 1916

In early January we joined the newly-formed 55th Division. We left Monchiet in the early afternoon and after a gruelling march along a pavé road slippery with mud and melted snow reached Beaumetz at night. The briefest halt and then on to Wailly, immediately behind the line some eight km south of Arras. From there we waded through a winding communication trench, a mile long but seemingly interminable. Liquid mud to the knees and bitterly cold sleet benumbed us through. At last we reached the Front line and took over from a French Territorial Regiment of Reservists.

Lt-Col Wainwright was in charge of the advance party that took over from the French Colonel and his staff. One night, long after the war, he told me of the shock he had when he saw the luxury they enjoyed in the local château they had made their headquarters. With great pride the French officer had shown him a bathroom lined with mirrors scrounged from wrecked houses. They were set round the walls at all angles, so that his lady friends could display their many charms in a state of total undress.

The whole trench system was in the most appalling condition. These were the worst trenches we had ever been in. No repairs had been done to them for months and months. At worst, they had collapsed inwards and did not give head shelter, at best they were a trough of liquid muck. This was a quiet part of the line and so repairs had never been done to the trenches. They were knee-deep in liquid mud. The dug-outs were foul and filthy. Sanitary discipline had been conspicuously absent. So during a February of driving snow and sleet we set about the distasteful task of cleaning out this Augean stable. Only the application of grease outwardly and rum inwardly saved us from frostbite and worse.

2
H

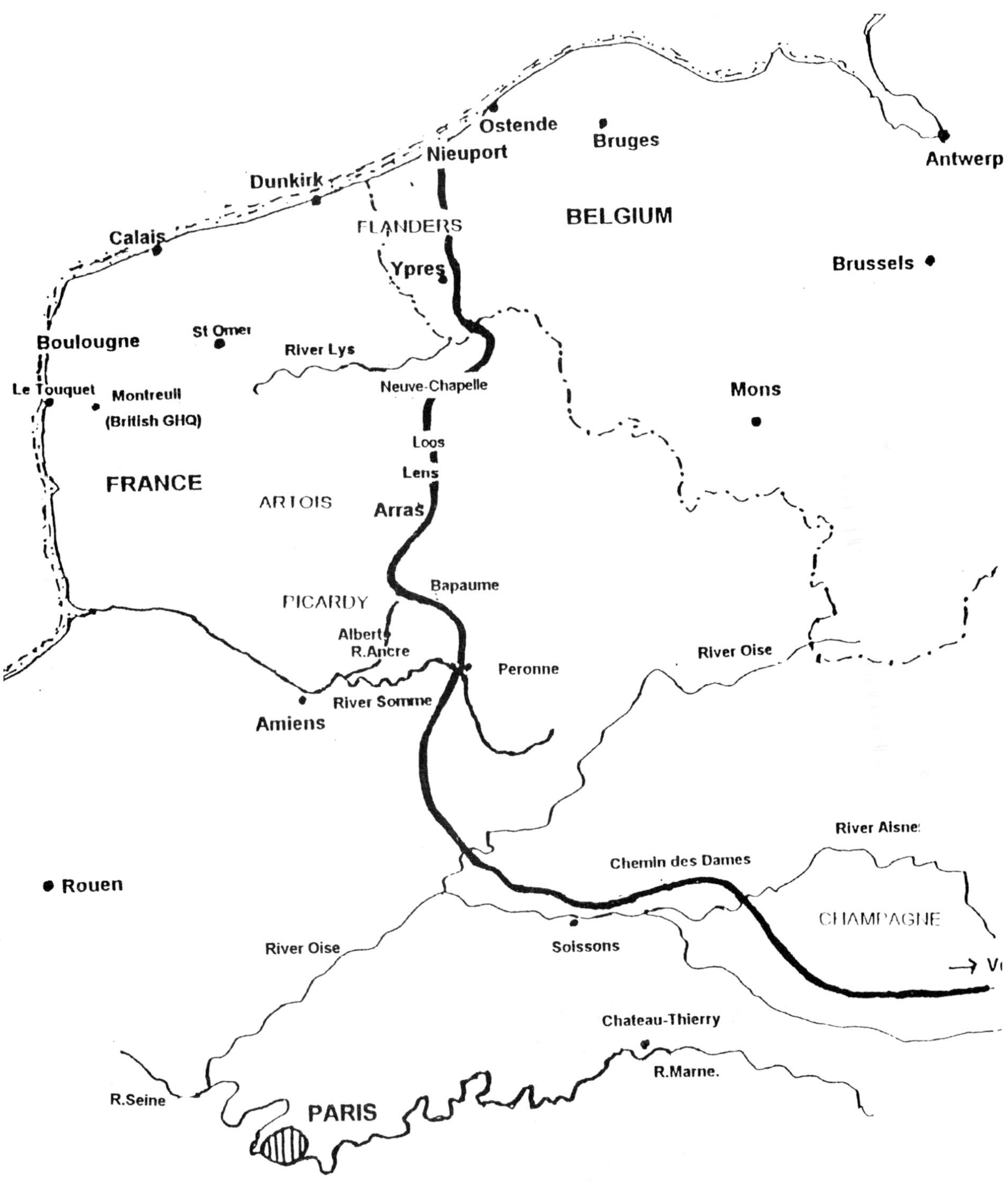

The Western Front 1916–1917.

Tunnelling. Part of the Grange subway, Vimy Ridge. 1996. Photo by Editor.

20 FEBRUARY 1916

H. and I were in the same traverse and went straight away on sentry duty. We were both too utterly fed up even to curse. Bodily exhausted, sodden and chilled to the bone with icy sleet; hungry and without rations or the means of lighting a fire to boil a dixie of water; not a dry square inch to sit upon, let alone a square foot of shelter beneath which to have the solace of a pipe. We agreed that this was the worst night of concentrated physical discomfort we had come across hitherto – and we were not strangers to discomfort.

Several hours of this misery passed and then an amazing change came over me. I became conscious, acutely conscious, that I was outside myself, that the real 'me' – the ego, spirit or what you like – was entirely separate and outside my fleshly body. I was looking in a wholly detached and impersonal way upon the discomforts of a khaki-clad body, which whilst I realised that it was my own, might easily have belonged to somebody else for all the direct connection I seemed to have with it. I knew that my body must be feeling acutely cold and miserable but I, my spirit part, felt nothing.

At the time it seemed a very natural happening, as the impossibilities of a dream seem right and natural to the dreamer, and it was only afterwards that I realised that I had been through one of the most wonderful experiences of my life.

In the morning H. remarked to me upon my behaviour during the night. For a long time I had been grimly silent and then had suddenly changed. My wit and humour in such trying circumstances had amazed him. I had chatted away as unconcernedly as if we had been warm and comfortable before a roaring fire. 'As if there was no war on' were his exact words I remember.

I never mentioned a word to H. or anybody else about my spiritual adventure that night. He would not have understood and would have laughed at it all, but nothing will shake my inward belief and knowledge that on this particular night my soul and body were entirely separated from each other.

22 FEBRUARY 1916. A PART-WRECKED BREWERY, WAILLY

I returned this afternoon from a six days' spell in the trenches. As far as activity goes they are the quietest I have ever been in, but they are very wet and the weather has been perfectly hellish of late. Today it is a raging snowstorm and extremely cold. I am feeling quite fit on it however. We are provided in the trenches with rubber thigh boots which reach almost to the waist, sort of sewerman's 'Wellingtons' and very useful too.

3 MARCH 1916. AN OUTHOUSE, BEAUMETZ-LES-LOGES

At last I have an opportunity of writing to you as we have just returned for a rest after a considerable spell in the trenches. During this time the weather has been abominable, very severe frosts and snow followed by a rapid thaw, with the result that we are now up to the eyes in mud and slush.

15 MARCH 1916. A DISUSED SHIPPON, WAILLY

During the last two days we have had a complete change in the weather. Up to that time it was terrible, snow and frost until we were frozen to the marrow. Today, however, the sun was so hot that we are all sunburnt, and have had to keep in the shade. I got a touch of frostbite in my right big toe, but four days massage and light duties put it right again. The pain was very severe whilst the circulation was returning.

I am writing this in the ruined village of Wailly. The inhabitants have long since fled inland. It has been very badly knocked about, indeed I do not think there is a single cottage which has not received some damage. As is usual extra special attention has been paid by Fritz to the church, reduced to a slender minaret rising above a sea of rubble.

You wonder sometimes if all this senseless damage can ever be repaired. Even before re-building could be started, removing the debris would take years. Personally I do not think these ruined places will ever be more than a rendezvous for Cook's tourists or film directors seeking good local colour for their plots.

I have noticed particularly an increase in the number of smaller birds, warblers etc. They are all in fine mating plumage and extremely active, hunting for nesting sites. In No-Man's Land in front of us, I have seen a covey of partridge quietly feeding notwithstanding the fire which passed over their heads. I suppose it is about the safest place where they could not be flushed by human beings.

We now have shrapnel-proof steel helmets and look like a gang of Chinese coolies or tea planters. They are somewhat heavy but delightfully cool.

The village of Wailly was to be in our care for the next six months. During our stay we strongly fortified the place with hidden machine-gun positions, surprise trenchers and barbed wire. Most of the village was well within machine-gun range and was an easy target for artillery, yet despite an occasional outburst of 'hate', it was a cushy and interesting job infinitely to be preferred to Front line duty.

From Wailly a road led straight through our lines and those of the enemy. Some distance along it, a screen made of straw was suspended across it on two high poles to prevent the enemy looking straight up the village street. McGivering and I had a special duty allocated to us. If the enemy broke through, we had to rush to this screen, deluge it with a tin of petrol we kept handy for that purpose, and set it alight. On many a night when artillery exchanges were more lively than usual, Mac and I would crouch in a little dug-out by the screen with the precious tin of petrol, wondering if this was to be our night or not.

13 APRIL 1916. THE KEEP, WAILLY

This place is simply overrun with cats. There are literally dozens of them. The originals, the fireside tabbies left behind when the inhabitants fled, are semi-wild, but their offspring are as wild and ferocious as young tigers. It is a curious thing how the habits of many generations of civilised life can be so rapidly changed when necessity makes them revert to the original wild state. These cats hunt and stalk the fiercest rats and there are some whoppers as large as rabbits. We regularly see some tough scraps between them. I don't suppose I overestimate if I put down the rat population of this village at a quarter million.

Everywhere is honeycombed with their burrows until the whole place is one gigantic warren of runs and holes. When the war is over the rat problem will prove a difficult task to tackle. At dusk we often have a good night's sport 'strafing' the rats with sticks. Spring has burst upon us suddenly and has come to stay. Sheltered pear and fruit trees are now in full blossom and everything is delightfully fresh and green.

27 APRIL 1916

The weather is beautiful and very hot, in fact just like English mid-summer. Here, however, it is only spring weather and it will become much warmer later on. The change of season took place in one day. We awoke one morning to find the swallows, martins and swifts here, and the trees bursting into green leaf. I suppose in hotter tropical countries the change comes even more quickly. In our debris-littered remnant of a garden there is a solitary apple tree. Great clusters of blossom like whity-pink bee swarms well nigh bend its boughs to the ground, but as yet there is not a single green leaf visible. A most curious yet delightful sight.

The warmth has also greatly increased the number of birds, many of them no doubt late migrants passing through, but still the increase is most marked. I heard the cuckoo early the other morning. There have been several troops of chattering jays about; their life at present seems to be an everlasting quarrel with the magpies over nesting sites. The magpie is by far the commonest bird round here. They are more numerous than the sparrows.

Nature seems to have accounted for the immense armies of vermin and small life that have bred unchecked by a corresponding increase in the number of hawks. A favourite trick of the latter is to skim along in a long volplane the whole length of an empty trench which of course simply swarms with mice and such like tit-bits.

The swallows have already set about building. From their point of view this land must be Utopia, *'beaucoup'* mud and *'beaucoup'* empty barns and outhouses. At night a large owl flits around. I imagine his waistcoat is sleek and well filled too.

The other day I was interested to notice the effect of noise – artillery fire – on the animal life. The majority simply paid no heed to the noise, the exceptions being cats and spiders. The cats immediately dived for the nearest cover, the spiders stiffened and shammed death, and if in the act of spinning, broke their thread and dropped to the ground. Beetles are not in the least sensitive.

Tin Hats sketch, drawn by Ellison after their issue at Wailly, probably in preparation for the Battle of the Somme. March 1916.

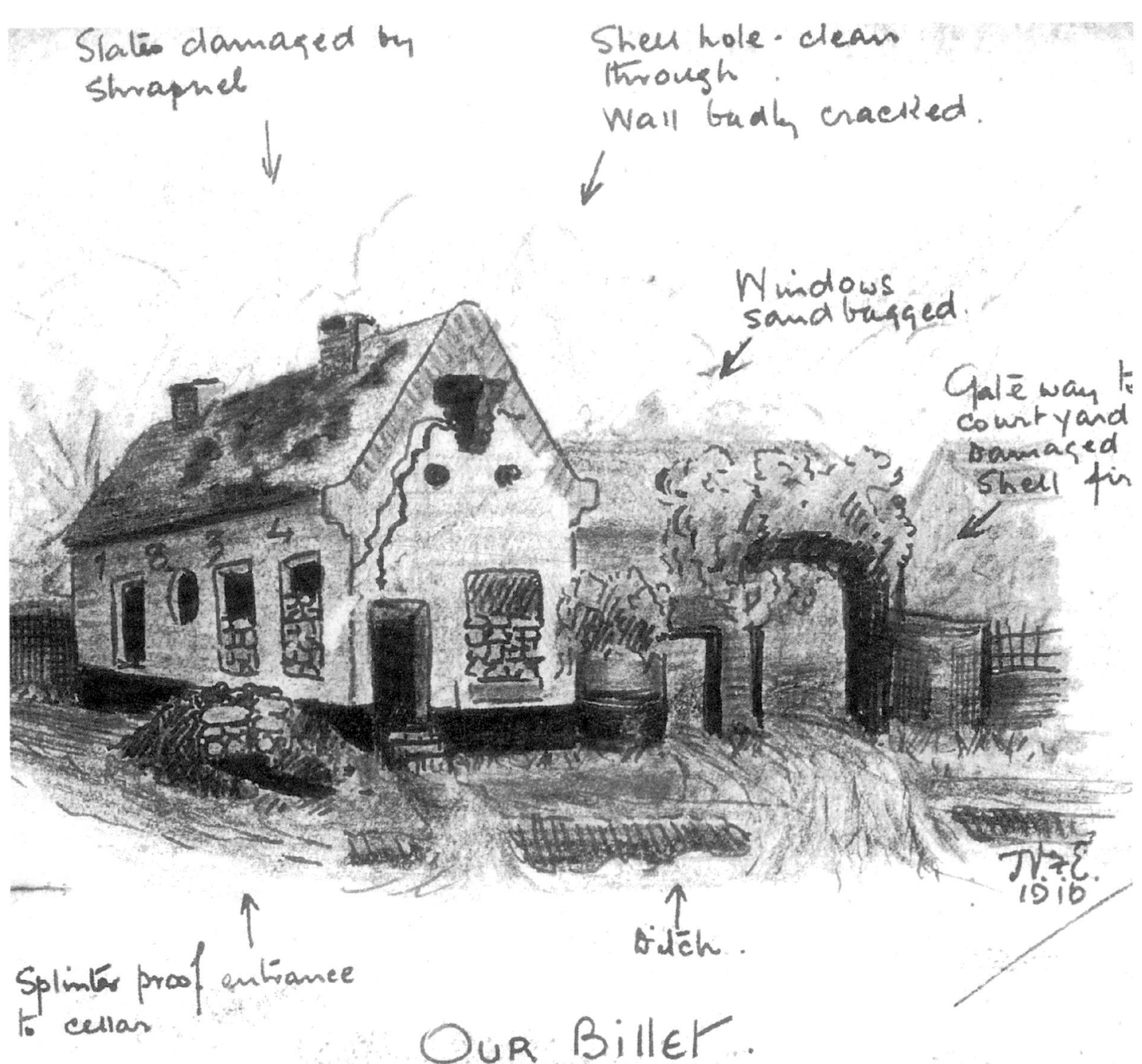

Wailly Keep. Colour sketch by N. Ellison. March 1916.
A farm-house at the village cross-roads we turned into a strong point. We lived in the cellar, proof against splinters but not shell-fire. As I dare not send this sketch in a letter home, I kept it in my pocket-book for over twelve months – hence its dog-eared appearance.

9 MAY 1916

Yesterday I had to go into the next village, Riviere, with a message. The inhabitants of a large number of them are still there although it is under a mile to the Front line trenches. Occasionally they get a dose of shells from Fritz, but that does not seem to worry them overmuch. They just carry on calmly tilling their little bits of soil and milking the cows. I went into one estaminet and, in conversation with the proprietor's daughter, was shown a mirror on the wall badly cracked by a shrapnel bullet that had come through one of the window panes. They appeared quite pleased with their 'souvenir' as they termed it.

Truly the sang-froid these French peasants exhibit, by sticking to their homes until the very last moment, is one of the most amazing things I have struck in an altogether amazing war. The countryside now looks at its best. When I tell you that I had not been out of this shell-wrecked village or seen a civilian for six weeks, you will realise how much I enjoyed this little jaunt into the borders of civilisation.

Colour sketch by Ellison. Sunrise and battleplanes.
My father was a very sick man and so, to keep him interested, I tried to include a rough sketch with every letter I sent home. The caption on the back of this one, reads – 'We had a very vivid sunrise the other morning. The whole sky and horizon was a deep orange slashed with bars of vermilion. Presently four of our battle planes sailed overhead in perfect formation towards the Jerry lines. On their right flank, two smaller and faster scouts kept worrying up and down. The whole convoy ploughed clean through this red sea of cloud, their under-planes occasionally a blood red. When I got back to the billet I hunted round for odd bits of pencil etc. and voici! the result. This impression however, conveys little idea of the rugged beauty of the original scene.' N.F.E.

Colour sketch by Ellison. Balloon sketch.

Opposite: Colour sketch by Ellison. Brasshat.

"BRASS HAT."
W.F.E.
-1916-

One of the most pitiful sights you come across out here in the line is the vast quantity of agricultural machinery lying about in the last stages of rust and decay. Piles of debris and rubble which were once houses leave me unmoved, but one of these cutter-cum-binder machines, a veritable work of art slowly falling into bits through sheer inattention, makes me angry and murmur hymns of hate under my breath. Really a funny thing that this should irritate one. Such a drop in the ocean in a war where the damage must be incalculable. At home I have seen people similarly annoyed at flowers being trampled underfoot, or fine old trees being cut down.

For bravado and pure cheek the cocky sparrow takes a lot of beating. In a very exposed position constantly under shell-fire stands a tall tree broken clean in half by a direct hit from a shell. In the jagged splinters at the top, sparrows have built their nests and, judging from the twitterings have successfully reared their broods of young.

Quite recently a nightingale has arrived in our neighbourhood. As a northerner I ought to be

The Somme battlefield.

Bringing up rations on the Somme.

charmed with its singing, but I am much disappointed. This bird certainly gets out a few sweet trills occasionally, but most of its song consists of hoarse garglings and burblings as if his throat was confoundedly sore. The corncrake has also made himself heard – his hoarse rattle blends beautifully with the machine-guns!

5 JUNE 1916. THE KEEP, WAILLY

On the whole, things are fairly quiet although the general tone is brisker. The night before last was decidedly breezy.

We had a very good sermon from the Brigade padre last Sunday; he is a good speaker and a man – which is the main point. He is a Liverpool man of the name of Matthews. After service I took communion. Our church is a shrapnel-riddled barn full of building swallows. We were heavily shelled during the service; several shells fell so near at one time, we feared we should have to abandon it. Anyhow we didn't.

Ever since I have been out here I have been immensely interested in the work of the Royal Engineers – the handy-men of the army. The result is that I have a practical knowledge of trench construction, revetting, sandbagging, barbed wiring, loop holing, draining and rough joinery.

McGivering and I have just built our OC a dug-out twelve feet underground, complete with glass doors and cemented brick floor. We also made all the furniture, four-poster bed with wire mattress, chair and two tables. We put our backs into the job and are proud of the results. The OC is very bucked about it and it is quite the show place of the village.

I do not mention this in any boastful spirit but simply to show you that I have learned my job well. I have always been a believer in every man, rich or poor, having a trade in his hands in addition to a profession in his head.

In the clay court yard of our billet we have laid out a six-hole putting course and have great sport with it. The clubs are a source of wonder and uncertainty to players and spectators alike.

12 JUNE 1916

One wonders if this disgusting cloud of pessimism will ever be lifted from England. For many months now we have been fed up with the whining tone adopted by the press. I suppose they will celebrate peace itself in sackcloth and ashes. Kitchener's death is a very real loss but he had sown his seed and it will make little difference. Pity is that he did not live long enough to reap the harvest.

Mac and I have been very busy as usual. We have just finished a topping little funk-hole for eight of us. An underground cellar it is, and we have lined it with wire bunks two high: quite ship-shape and cosy. At the end of the war I expect a funk-hole at the bottom of the lawn will be more fashionable than the old type of rustic summer house.

Most of the swallows have hatched their broods now and are busy hunting food for them.

In the middle of April spring burst upon us with amazing suddenness. In a day it seemed, the swallows and warblers arrived from the south, and the fruit blossom opened and clothed poor battered Wailly with an appealing beauty. The night was filled with the song of nightingales. I cannot recollect any spring that thrilled me more. One felt that man might destroy himself and his civilisation through the incredible stupidity of war, but the annual re-birth of nature would continue. Here was something assured and permanent: an established truth in a world of constantly alternating values.

But the comparative quietness of Wailly was too good to last; things started to ginger up and before long, rumours became general of a great offensive, to break the deadlock of trench warfare before the winter weather sets in. We were being prepared for our share in it.

Rumours became reality when, following a week's artillery bombardment of a concentrated intensity such as before had never been known, in the early morning of 1 July 1916, the British attacked along a twenty-mile front on the Somme area. By nightfall, the total of our casualties was staggering, but let me quote from Winston Churchill's *The World Crisis, 1916–1918:*

> 'July 1st. Night closed on the still thundering battlefield. Nearly 60,000 British soldiers had fallen. This was the greatest loss and slaughter sustained in a single day in the whole history of the British Army. Of the infantry who advanced to the attack, nearly half had been overtaken by death, wounds, or capture. Against this . . . we had gained 4,000 prisoners and a score of cannon. In these siege offensives, which occupied the years 1915, 1916 and 1917, the French and British Armies suffered nearly double the casualties inflicted on the Germans . . . British casualties were never less than 3 to 2 and often nearly double the corresponding German losses. The losses of the Germans from 1915 to 1917 were considerably less than their annual intake of young men reaching military age.'

The bravery of the German soldier behind a machine-gun in a concrete pill-box beat us; after months of mad fury and prodigious expenditure of human life, the battle petered out. The mud won: it brought both sides to a standstill.

In the quietness of Wailly we heard the ceaseless thundering cannonade to the southwards. We read in the newspapers from home of our amazing 'successes' – a quarter mile of trench taken here, a few yards bite into his line there, but no mention of the cost. Our turn would come soon enough. We knew that much.

20 JULY 1916

We left Wailly and by daily marches under a tropical sun reached the battle area. The night of 28 July saw us sleeping in a wood, Bois de Tailles, near Bray. The actual fighting was only a few miles away; the sky was lit up by gunfire; the volume of sound was menacing.

It now became necessary to take stock of my personal position. I had been away from home for two years, during which period I had visited it three times on leave, once for four days, and twice for ten. For eighteen months I had been a Front-line soldier and physically, was a very tired man; perhaps more important in the long run, I was a very worried man. My father never fully recovered from my mother's death and his health became gradually worse. Letters from home are one of the bright spots on active service, but now when one came not addressed in his writing, I opened it anxiously, for I always feared that it might contain the worst possible news. I had scrapped my commission papers, refused promotion twice and could see no end to this dreary war.

Luck had been with me so far, and now came another slice which was to alter the whole war for me. So many battalions had been completely obliterated in this shambles that there remained no nucleus about which each might be re-formed. In consequence, a certain proportion of men was ordered to remain behind at the transport lines when the battalion went into action. I was told off for this 'lifeboat party' as we called it, and no man was more thankful. I acted as company storeman, delivering rations and mail, unloading wagons, cooked for the boys 'up there', and did a hundred and one jobs

Next page: The road to Guillemont. 11 September 1916. Q1163.

4 SEPTEMBER 1916. DERNANCOURT (BILLETED IN A SLAUGHTERHOUSE)

I do not suppose I am giving anything away if I just mention that we have been in the Big Push as the newspapers like to call it. You people at home have no idea what an enormous power artillery fire wields in this war. I have seen German Front-line trenches that have been so smashed and pounded that they are now little better than plough furrows.

You will be interested to hear that our Engineers have built a new railway here, and named one of the stations Edge Hill.

We left the Somme at the end of September 1916, and returned to Ypres, to a flattened city little more than a heap of rubble. I was still with the commisariat but never went beyond the support trenches. Going up with the transport at night was usually a nasty business as all roads in the Salient were regularly shelled.

CHAPTER TEN

BACK TO YPRES

Returning to Ypres, Ellison describes a Christmas Eve visit to Poperinghe, a major rest centre for British troops, with its cafes and estaminets. When visiting Poperinghe alone, Ellison used to visit Talbot House (Toc H), which still survives today.

Oliver Lyttleton (Viscount Chandos) who served in Flanders as a subaltern in the Grenadier Guards writes in his book, From Peace to War, *'When we relieved troops in the Front line we used to go by train from Poperinghe to the base of the Salient'. Unfortunately 'the Germans had a tactless habit of shelling Poperinghe railway station with a high velocity naval-gun ; its shells gave no notice of their arrival'.*

Edmund Blunden in Undertones of War *describes his move north in December 1916 after the Somme offensive, to a camp a mile or less from the road to Poperinghe. 'One of our first impressions here was caused by the prominent notices against the Post Office (open!) concerning gas and the state of the wind; the skeleton of Ypres thus began to give us a nudge and a whisper'.*

In the Middle Ages, Poperinghe was a member of the Hanseatic League and an important cloth-trading town. It is the most important hop-growing area (the Hoppelandes) in Belgium. During the very severe winter of 1916–17, Norman Ellison contracted Trench foot, a kind of massive chilblain due to the restriction of circulation in cold and damp. It had caused serious problems the previous winter amongst soldiers in the Ypres Salient.

6 OCTOBER 1916. THE RAMPARTS, YPRES

I have written you previous letters from many queer spots but the place where this is being written certainly takes the biscuit. I am way down underground in a wooden walled alcove off a long tunnel splendidly lit by electric light and as snug and cosy as could be. Up above are the ruins and debris of a once very fine city, Ypres, now so badly battered and bashed about that it is scarcely recognisable. I have many happy memories of it in the early days of the war, but now it is a nightmare.

I am keeping as fit as a fiddle. Some little time back I got a bad chill and my temperature went up to 102 degrees, but a day's rest put me as right as rain again. A bitter wind has been blowing across the Flanders plain for weeks on end and it seems we shall never be properly warm again. A mug of hot tea left out in the open was frozen solid within minutes. Transport men were ordered to walk alongside their horses as riders had been frozen to death in the saddle. We endured 12–15 degrees of frost, whilst according to the newspapers, London had one degree and the provinces five degrees.

21 DECEMBER 1916. TRANSPORT LINES, OUTSIDE POPERINGHE

A letter I wrote to my sister from the transport lines outside Poperinghe makes interesting reading today:

'I will send you some more hand-made lace, as soon as I have the chance of going to the cottage where I bought the last lot. I do not think I have described these cottages to you.

'They are really tumbledown shacks built mostly of old packing cases and roofed with beaten-out biscuit tins. The interior is generally furnished in the crudest way imaginable: all home-made

Toc H. Poperinghe. 1996. Photo by Editor.

furniture with perhaps an occasional household treasure snatched up in the hurried flight from the wreck of their homes.

'These people are all refugees and have suffered greatly; yet with amazing sang-froid which we used to reckon as being essentially British, they are happy in having homes at all. For the most part, the young men are away with the re-organised Belgian Army, so the whole business of running the household falls on the shoulders of the women; and most capable they are too.

'Every hut caters for the troops with coffee, fried eggs and chips. One cannot help thinking that the arms of the new Belgium (*après la guerre*) must embody some hint of this national dish. Say: *oeufs couchant* surmounted by chips rampant on a ground, café.

'Further, they eke out a living by selling all sorts of odds and ends. Many is the rugged shanty that has an embryo Harrod's hidden beneath its Huntley and Palmer's roof.

'Ceilings and walls are thickly pasted with old newspapers, artistic tastes being sacrificed to warmth. As a result you see *John Bull* nestling cheek by jowl with *The Methodist Preacher*, and the *Daily Mail* partly obliterated by *Comic Cuts*.

'In their spare time, and heaven knows how they find it, the women make lace, a vastly complicated business of hundreds of pins hedgehog-like on a board and countless threads on coloured bobbins. A rapid Cinquevallian shuffling and juggling, a tug here, a twist there and 'presto!', the delicate tracery of a spider's web grows before your eyes. It always amazes me how a tousled, top-heavy, splaw-footed thing in uncouth sabots, can turn out such lovely intricate work. More wonderful still is the way they manage to keep it clean amid the mud and filthy surroundings of a century-old hen-roost.

'Young and old speak tolerably good English; also many English words they should not know.

'This lace cost me two and a half francs per Belgian yard (seven-tenths of a metre or roughly twenty-eight inches). This same lace is being sold in the large towns at eight francs per yard. I was in Poperinghe the other night and saw some genuine hand-made Brussels lace at two hundred and fifty francs per metre. It was most beautiful work.'

26 DECEMBER 1916

I have not yet received any Christmas letters but as there has been a severe gale blowing on and off for the last few days, I've no doubt that accounts for the delay. I have had a jolly Christmas: plenty to eat and drink, impromptu sing-songs and fun in general. I spent Christmas Eve in the neighbouring town (Poperinghe), had a rattling good feed and finished up with a visit to the cinema-cum-music hall show. Very good it was too.

This writing is somewhat erratic, but my fingers are half frozen with cold as there is a severe frost outside. The recent gale has done a lot of damage with cottages, bivouacs and sheds blown down. We had a large tarpaulin which must have weighed

Photo taken at Poperinghe in November 1916 to send home as Christmas card. Norman Ellison, George Lowes and Arnold Flint (standing) and Jim Brown (sitting) – all Liverpool Rifles.

half a ton, ripped to ribbons as it roofed a shed.

It would have done you good to have seen the troops doing their Christmas shopping in Poperinghe. With no females to restrain them, they bought the place out, walking about laden with oranges, holly, sides of pork, geese, vegetables and many other delicacies. No doubt about it, it takes more than a war to damp the spirits of the boys. Genuine English Bass was also on sale and went with a bang.

At night the estaminets supplied their patrons with cigars and crackers. It makes you forget the war to see seasoned soldiers playing the goat in coloured paper hats or rendering unsought for solos on a one-note whistle.

Occasionally I visited Poperinghe alone, when I always spent some time at Talbot House, or 'Toc H' as we called it. In a mad world it was an oasis of quiet and I used to look forward to an hour or two of peace there, reading a book or writing letters. The most important place in the house was a chapel in the upper room, an attic that ran the full length of the building, and originally used for storing dried hops. The altar was a carpenter's bench which had been found in the garden. On either side stood a great candlestick made out of an old carved bed-post by a Canadian Gunner. To attend a service in such plain and simple surroundings was an inspiration, far more appealing than any church parade, or so it seemed to me. Toc H was one of the good things that came out of the war and persisted. Today its branches are in many parts of the world.

We entered 1917 still half frozen. I was feeling the winter acutely and realised that my strength was slowly ebbing. My name was on the leave-list for late January, so I determined to stick it out. Two of my toes became frostbitten and started to turn black. My leave was only three days away, but my foot was so swollen I could not get the boot off. At last came my leave warrant and a chit to be signed that I had taken a bath and was free of lice. I certainly could not have a bath in a boot, but I found a way of getting that chit signed and set off home. It was a nightmare journey. Walking was agony, but I knew if any Medical Officer spotted me hobbling along, I would be sent to hospital right away. So I marched with the rest of them and at last reached home.

The toes were now largely black jelly and my father called in the family doctor. He would have nothing to do with the matter and so I reported to the nearest military hospital, the Wallasey Town Hall Military Hospital, and asked for an extension of my leave. They took me in at once, put me to bed and there I remained for several weeks. My campaigning days were over, although I did not know it at the time.

I shall always remember my stay at the Wallasey Town Hall Military Hospital with deep affection. For two years I had known practically nothing of bodily cleanliness, properly cooked food or physical relaxation. Suddenly I found myself again living a civilised life. The sheer animal pleasure of sleeping between clean sheets, of being looked after by kindly people concerned with the preservation of life, rather than the spreading of death, I find impossible to describe in words. I lay there in bed utterly content with all my immediate worries cast away as a snake sloughs off its old skin. I thought then and still think, it was as near to heaven-on-earth as one could ever hope to find in this life.

In due course I was passed out by a medical board as fit for a spell of convalescence at Southport. When I left Wallasey I took with me not only the happiest memories, but also two friendships that, despite the vicissitudes of forty years, have lasted to this day. Sister Margaret Smith-Hills nursed me back to health: with George Preston, a fellow patient I discovered common interests that time has not exhausted. Life for the soldier when he once reaches hospital is a series of medical boards until he is marked fit for active service, placed in a home service category or discharged to civilian life. I knew that I could not withstand the rigours of another winter at the Front, and, fortunately for me, the final board

Sister Margaret Smith-Hills– dedicatee.

before which I appeared thought likewise. The year slipped by and then on 27 December 1917 my father died suddenly in his chair. I had to orientate my life anew.

On 11 November 1918 an Armistice was signed and we knew the war was over. Manchester went completely wild that day. No trams were running and all the pubs were closed. Piccadilly and the main thoroughfares were tightly jammed with cheering crowds. It was pandemonium. One incident has remained in my memory, two sailors jigging on the roof of a taxicab when it collapsed and they disappeared inside.

In February 1920 I was demobilised. It was a strange and unsettling experience to be my own master again after four and a half years of discipline. I had to find 'diggings', buy a complete rig-out of civilian clothing and get down to a job. But I was free at last and that was all that mattered. So with a little under a hundred pounds in my pocket I started a new life.

I returned to a business world very different from the one I had left in 1914. During the war years too much money had been made far too easily by those who had been classed as 'indispensable'. Mediocrity was now in power with money the god to be worshipped. The finest young men of my generation had volunteered and been killed in the Ypres Salient and later on in the senseless slaughter of the Somme and Paschendaele battles. The return of the ex-serviceman was vaguely resented. No doubt he could be fitted in somehow, somewhere, but . . . It took me sometime to settle down to this new world of discontent and disillusionment. My home had gone, so had my prospective job in Hamburg, but deliberately I refrained from comparisons, from striking the balance of a personal profit and loss account of what the war had cost me. No good could come from so doing, only unhappiness. What is more I have never done so. Not even today when I can look back on those early struggles in a wholly detached way. My most pressing need was to earn enough money to keep myself and my sisters in rooms. I joined an uncle in his firm of wholesale paper merchants in Liverpool.

Eventually my sisters struck out on their own. Dorothy who was a Red Cross nurse went to that wonderful hospital at Eltham where those who had suffered severe facial wounds had their faces rebuilt. My younger sister, Winifred went to Paris, took a diploma in hairdressing and then obtained a good post in Johannesburg.

A Memory of Christmas 1915. Colour sketch by N. Ellison drawn soon after being demobilised.

Blighty. Colour sketch by Norman Ellison. 1920.

CHAPTER ELEVEN

POSTSCRIPTS: NEWSPAPER ARTICLES ALONG THE ROAD TO POP

A SOLDIER REVISITS A LAND OF GHOSTS: SOME MEMORIES OF A TRAGIC PILGRIMAGE

In appearance it is only a very ordinary road, straight as a die with a border of erect poplar trees accompanying it from start to finish. Probably you would find its exact counterpart a dozen times within a search of a twenty miles radius. Yet to those who soldiered in the Ypres Salient – their number must be hundreds of thousands – the road to Poperinghe or 'Pop' road is as familiar and as unforgettable as the Strand or Piccadilly.

It is the only main road which leads rearwards from Ypres, and so it became the main artery which pumped an endless stream of men, guns, shells, rations, and a thousand other things into the hungry maw of the Salient. All day it slept peacefully in the sunlight, little disturbed by the small parties who brazenly tramped its surface. But at dusk the road woke up, and by dark it had become a turbid stream of humanity and horses, motors and mules, with a forward current and a rearward current jostling each other in its narrow breadth.

Occasional bursts of shrapnel would stab the darkness and whine amongst the tree branches. A few gaps in the stream of men, a temporary stoppage to drag the injured to the roadside, a little congestion and a deal of swearing, and the stream would roll on as slowly and surely as if nothing had ever happened, until the first streaks of dawn flushed the sky.

Such was the 'Pop' road I knew – knew well, every stick and stone, gatepost and tree, so many times I had slogged along its ill-set pavé.

Substantially I found it the same old road I had hankered after. True, it had been re-metalled in places and dozens of unpretentious erected while-you-wait shacks squatted in the neighbouring fields, but the old familiar landmarks still met me on my tramp and jogged the mind back in an instant to those stirring days when their advent conveyed a more significant meaning.

Presently came Vlamertinghe, new risen from her ruins with workmen putting the finishing touches to the church spire. Adjoining the church is a large military cemetery, the first one to be finally completed. The many thousands of plain headstones, row upon row set in the greenest of close-cropped turf with beds of brilliant and sweet-smelling flowers, give the enclosure a dignity and sacredness which could not be surpassed.

On the road again, past the watering tanks and the large mill which was used as a dressing-station until a half-hour's tramp brought me to the straggling village of Brandhook, once the centre of a dozen or more rest camps snug hid in the thick copses which encircle the place. It seemed strangely silent and deserted now, for my memories were of crowds of khaki, laughter and light and oh! blended warmth and all the comforts of 'home' that really matter. After the miseries of the trenches this was really 'home'. Here the iron grip of self relaxed, and men became civilised beings again for the brief period of their rest. Of necessity the hub of all this social revival was the local auberge with the large dancing room and execrable piano.

Even if the heat had not proved so physically insistent, 'old time's sake' would have driven me to its inviting door. The same bare room and crude bar counter, the same battered piano and, miracles never end, the same buxom Marie smiling a welcome!

She did not remember me personally – how was that possible when ten million troops had crossed her threshold? – but she knew the regiment and we talked with the happiness that comes with the unexpected meeting of old friends again.

From here to Poperinghe every yard of the countryside brought back old memories with a rush.

Tiny cottages where we had bartered 'bully' for hand-made lace or a feed of eggs and chips; the lane leading through the hop plantation to our old transport lines (what a row there was when some of those hop-poles went for firewood); the short cut across the fields to dodge the 'red caps' when we had visited Pop passless; the tapering archery pole and the railway station at the entrance to the town, the crooked narrow streets with the same old shops and the same splay-footed inhabitants.

Across the Grande Place – once a fair target for long-distance shooting – to a restaurant where I had celebrated my first leave with a memorable feed of duck and green peas and champagne: I dined there well.

Curiosity must need lead me to the old furniture depository which the Divisional Concert Party had turned into an excellent theatre. Many the night we had forgotten the war in the topical humour and broad farce we had enjoyed there. An enjoyment nonetheless, even when abruptly interrupted by the order, 'All lights out', and the German planes high above commenced to drop 'eggs' all over the town. Now it has reverted to its original prosaic use.

What more fitting than I should return to Ypres by railway along the identical line which five years ago we traversed at night, lightless and at snail's pace with our engine smothered beneath a tarpaulin to hide the tell-tale glare from the fire-box.

N.F.E.
Liverpool Echo, 2 May 1924,
by Norman F. Ellison

LIVERPOOL 'RIFLES' RE-UNION

WAR-TIME MEMORIES REVIVED

It is just 21 years ago, this weekend, since the majority of Liverpool's Territorial units set sail for the theatres of war in France. Most of them were youngsters full of the spirit of adventure, and many of them lived through nearly four years of untold horrors and privations, for the Liverpool troops took part in most of the great battles.

On Friday evening 300 Officers and men of the 'Liverpool Rifles' (6th Rifle Batt. The King's Regt), who had sailed for France in the steamship *City of Edinburgh*, 21 Feb, 1915, attended a re-union at Reece's Cafe, Clayton Square. The ship that carried them has long been broken up, but the great ship's bell, which is now a regimental trophy, hung before the chairman, Col J.B. McKaig, and was used to call the gathering to attention.

A letter was read from Sir Philip Gibbs. He wrote:

> 'May I send a few words of greeting to the Liverpool Rifles at their re-union. Some of them will remember a small-sized war correspondent who came to visit them in the line during the Great War. I well remember coming to see you at a place called Vaux-sur-Somme, which was a kind of outpost, only divided from the enemy by a wooden drawbridge, and some marshy ground. There was a sentry called Ellison with whom I talked, and I rather fancy that some of you wore green veils over your faces for camouflage purposes, but that may only be a trick of memory. Anyhow the Liverpool Rifles were there conducting a kind of old-fashioned warfare of a more gentlemanly kind than usual in that part of the world.

The Liverpool "Rifles" went into worse

> places than that, such as the boggy ground of Flanders, when it was an abomination of desolation. They made a great name for themselves in history, and I am proud of having recorded some of their deeds. We are all getting older now, but the spirit of comradeship remains as the only good memory of that war.'

Norman Ellison, who with Russell Anderson, organised the re-union, was the sentry named by Sir Philip Gibbs. A souvenir programme designed by Mr Ellison, and containing photographs of Vaux and the marshes was presented to each guest.

Liverpool Express, 23 February 1936, by Lewis Gunn

GENTLEMANLY WAYS OF WARFARE

From the 'Daily Post' and 'Daily Chronicle' Special Correspondent, Philip Gibbs. General Headquarters. October 10th

Two days ago I had an adventure which still seems to me unreal and fantastic. I went into a village held by British troops beyond our line of trenches, with nothing dividing them from the enemy but a little undergrowth. And the queerest part of the adventure was the sense of safety, the ridiculously false security with which we could wander about the village and up the footpath beyond, with the knowledge that one's movements were being watched by German eyes, and that the whole place could be blown off the face of the earth but for the convenient fact that the Germans who were living in the village beyond the footpath were under our own observation and at the mercy of our own guns.

SOMETHING EXTRAORDINARY

To those who do not know at first hand the conditions of life along the greater part of the Western Front, it is difficult to explain the sense of stupefaction with which I was filled in this extraordinary place. I have said that it is beyond our lives. After a familiarity with the Ypres Salient and anywhere between the Yser Canal and the trenches at Neuve Chapelle for instance that sounds like a fairy tale. To go over the parapet of the first line of trenches, even to put one's head up for a single second, is to risk immediate death 'One asks for it' as soldiers say.

Beyond the first trench is the 'dead ground' where no life can exist, a blasted place, with a few hundred corpses, the churned up earth of mine craters and shell-holes. There are listening posts out there dug underground. Occasionally at night bold men will crawl out a little way on their stomachs, and lie 'doggo' simulating death with a very earnest realism, surprised after – if they had the luck to come back – that their pretence was not made perfect by a sniper's bullet or a bit of shell.

UNFAMILIAR SURROUNDINGS

That is the familiar way of things in this war, and, therefore, when I say that there is one village thrust out beyond our trenches, with no barrier of earthwork between the garrison and the enemy, I am saying an astounding thing, hardly credible to soldiers who have not seen it. Needless to say, it is not in the flat fields of Flanders, but where, in another part of the line men who have worked down from the deadly Salient of Ypres find hills again and village roads down which they may walk under steep bluffs, close, but invisible to the enemy, and stand on high ground, looking across to the enemy's trenches a mile or two away, perfectly outlined as though by a brush of white-wash on a background of green slopes. So that the veil which hides the enemy's position in Flemish fields is lifted at last, and the war zone is a wide panorama, across where one's glasses may sweep to watch the bursting shells or villages where Germans live, or even, as I saw two days ago, German soldiers themselves like little ants on the far ground.

I stood on a hill here with a French lieutenant and one of his men. The detachment itself was some distance away, but after an exchange of compliments in an idyllic glade, where a little party of French soldiers lived in the friendliest juxtaposition with the British infantry surrounding them – it was a cheery bivouac among the trees, with the fragrance of a stewpot mingled with the odour of burning wood – the lieutenant insisted upon leading the way to the top of the hill. He made a slight detour to point out a German shell which had fallen there without exploding, and made laughing comments upon the harmless, futile character of the Germans in front of us. 'They do their best to kill us, but oh so feebly.'

Yet when I took a pace towards the shell he called out sharply *'Non touchez pas'*. I would rather have touched a sleeping tiger than the conical piece of metal with its unexploded possibilities, but bent low to see the inscriptions on it scratched by French gunners with more recklessness of death. *'Mort aux boches'* was scrawled upon it between the men's initials

LOOKING DOWN ON ENEMY POSITION

Then we came to the hill crest and the last of our trenches, and, standing there, looked down upon two villages separated by a piece of marshy water. In the farthest village were Germans and in the nearest, just below us were, down the steep cliff, our own men.

Between the two there was a narrow causeway across the marsh, and a strip of woods half a rifle shot in length. Behind in a sweeping semicircle round their village and ours were the German trenches and the German guns. I looked into the streets of both villages as clearly as one may see into Clovelly village from the crest of the hill. In our own village a few British soldiers were strolling about. Others were sitting on the window-sill of a cottage knocking their heels.

In the German village the roadways were concealed by the perspective of the houses with their gables and chimney-stacks so that I could not see any passers-by. But at the top of the road going out of the village and standing outside the last house on the road was a solitary figure – a German sentry.

The French lieutenant pointed to a thin mast away from the village on the hillside. 'Do you see? That is their flagstaff. They hoist their flag for victory. It wagged a good deal during the recent Russian fighting, but lately, since our advance they have not had the cheek to put it up.' The cheery lieutenant laughed very heartily at that naked pole on the hill. Then I left him and joined our own men and went down a steep hill path into that strange village below, well outside our line of trenches and thrust forwards as an outpost in the marsh. German eyes could see me as I walked. At any moment these little houses about me might have been smashed into rubbish heaps. But no shell came to disturb the waterfowl among the reeds around.

CHIVALROUS EXCURSIONS

And so it is that the life in this place is utterly abnormal, and while the guns were silent except for long-range fire – an old-fashioned mode of war – what the adjutant of this little outpost calls a 'gentlemanly warfare' prevails. Officers and men sleep within a few hundred yards of the enemy. When a fight takes place, it is a chivalrous excursion such as Sir Walter Manny would have loved, between thirty and forty men on one side, against somewhat the same number on the other.

Our men steal out along the causeway which crosses the marsh – a pathway about four foot wide, broadening out in the middle, so that a little redoubt or blockhouse is established there. Then across a narrow drawbridge, then along the path again until they come to the thicket which screens the German village.

It sometimes happens, as the other night, that a party of Germans are creeping forward from the other direction in just the same way, disguised in parti-coloured clothes splashed with greens and reds and browns to make them invisible between the trees, with brown masks over their faces. Then suddenly contact was made. Into the silence of the wood comes the sharp crack of rifles, a zip-zip of bullets, the shouts of men who have given up the game of invisibility. It was a very sharp encounter the other night, and our men brought back many German helmets and other trophies as proof of victory. Then to bed in the village and a good night's rest as when English knights fought the French not far from these fields of war, chronicled in the chivalrous pages of that good storyteller, Sir John Froissart.

VISITS TO THE OUTPOSTS

Two days ago I went along the causeway and out into the wood where the outposts stood listening for any crack of a twig which might betray a German footstep. I was startled when I came upon the men suddenly, almost invisible against the tree trunks. And there they stood motionless with their rifles ready peering through the brushwood.

If I had followed the path on which they stood for just a little way I should have walked into the German village. But, on the other hand, I should not have walked back again.

When I left the village and climbed up the hill to our own trenches again, I laughed aloud at the fantastic visit to the grim little outpost in the marsh. If all the war was like this it would be a 'gentlemanly business' as the officer remarked, for one need not hide in holes in the earth nor crouch for three months below ground until there is an hour or two of massacre below a storm of high explosives. In the village on the marsh, men at least fight against other men, and not against invisible powers which belch forth death.

Daily Post, 16 October 1915.

P A R T   T W O

SELECTED LETTERS

Portrait of N. Ellison in 1971 when he was 78.

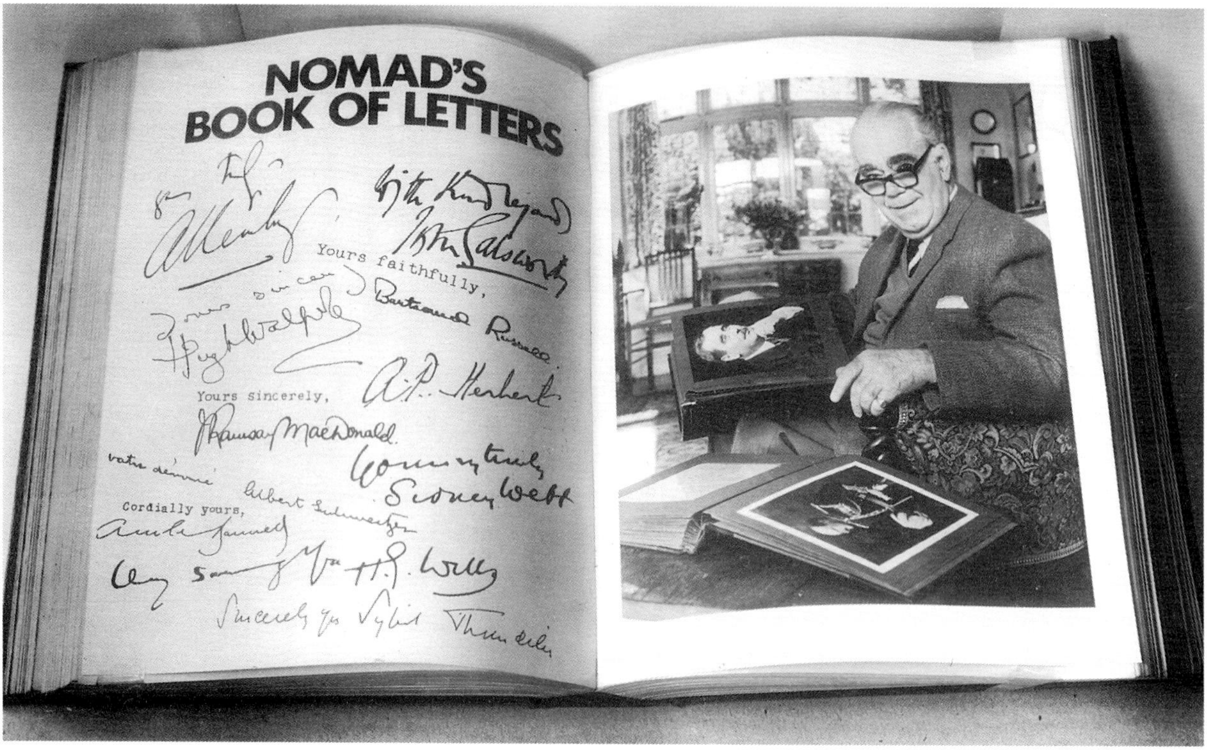

NOMAD'S BOOK OF LETTERS

Yours faithfully,

Yours sincerely,

Cordially yours,

TO PUBLISH OR NOT TO PUBLISH

The letters form an interesting and unique straw poll of a small cross-section of the intelligentsia of the period between the two world wars. In 1927, Norman Ellison, engaged in writing his diary, thought that the younger generation should be warned in no uncertain terms of the waste and horror of all warfare, but wondered whether or not his diary should be published. Close friends warned him that he would be trying to influence their minds before they were old enough to think for themselves, so he decided to write a letter to a few distinguished men posing his problem. Should he tell the younger generation the real truth about war as set down in his diary, or should war be glorified under the guise of patriotism, and his diary shelved?

LETTER WRITTEN BY NORMAN ELLISON TO 'OLDER AND MATURER MINDS', BETWEEN 1927 AND 1934

Dear Sir,

Red-hot patriotism rushed me into the war in August 1914 and – to cut a long story short – it was far from being a good war for me. To-day I am cooler and I hope wiser, and deep within me I feel that my sons and in turn, their sons, ought to be warned against the insensate waste and hellishness of all warfare. Solely with this object before me, I am typing out a diary of my war-time experiences – a true and honest account.

But I am encountering some opposition from elder members of the family, on the grounds that I shall prejudice the minds of my boys before they reach an age to judge for themselves; that it is 'unpatriotic', and so on. Am I doing the right thing or not?

I address this point blank question to you Sir, because I know you to be a man with the courage of his convictions upon this vital problem of patriotism versus war, and I would respect your opinion, and if I may ask for it – your advice.

In advance I wish to thank you for the kindness of your reply.

Yours faithfully,
Signed. N. F. Ellison.

In many cases the letter was further elaborated to suit the individual recipient. As Norman Ellison did not have any children of his own his reference to 'my boys' must have referred to young people in general, or at that time, to his possible future family. C.E. Montague of the *Manchester Guardian* replying on 7 July 1927, was sympathetic: 'In writing about the war as I saw it, a similar wish to protect my own five sons from illusions and sufferings was one of my strongest motives.' Ramsay MacDonald, the first Labour Prime Minister, in a letter dated 14 March 1927 wrote: 'I think that you are doing the right thing, in giving your family an absolutely unvarnished account of your experiences.'

Encouraged, Norman Ellison wrote to nearly eighty equally distinguished men and women. He received about sixty replies during the period 1927–34. Of those he contacted many were writers, some of whom referred him to their own books, or those by other writers that they admired. For example, Siegfried Sassoon mentions his own war poems written between 1915 and 1919, and recommends *Undertones of War* by Edmund Blunden, 'a sound book beautifully written by a man who always tells the truth'.

Edmund Blunden writes: 'I hope that you will not only type out but also print your exact account of your war.' However, he wonders whether it is possible to obtain the attention of the young generation: 'My book is read by older people almost entirely.' Both R.H. Mottram and C.E. Montague were happy to allow quotes from their works to be used in the diary but the Revd G.A. Studdert Kennedy ('Woodbine Willie') declined to provide a foreword to Ellison's war diary, suggesting instead that he should quote from his book, *The Hardest Part*. John Drinkwater replied: 'There are a great many young men and women today who remember nothing of the war, and unless education takes the matter very firmly in hand, we may in a few years time have a new generation beguiled by the old romantic frivolities about fighting. Man is not easily impressed by horrors that he has not experienced.' He enclosed three of his articles on the subject. A.P. Herbert raises the question: 'What is the truth? . . . And even from the trenches does one see the truth?' However, in principle he believes that Ellison's attitude is correct.

The philosopher Bertrand Russell writing from the progressive school he established in Petersfield, gives a very direct reply based on how he acted with his own children: 'No fact of any sort should be concealed from the young if their curiosity leads them to wish to know about it.' He was scathing about 'some pacifists who try to prevent children for as long as possible knowing that wars occur'. This he sees 'as quite as pernicious as the militarist teaching that wars are a kind of picnic'. The writer A.A. Milne is of like mind: 'I think it the duty of any parent to bring up his children with a realisation of the utter futility and wickedness of war.'

George Bernard Shaw believes 'anyone who produces a genuine record of the war is doing a public service'. Hugh Walpole opposes war, but believes in defending ourselves against aggression: 'War is damnable – a crime except in defence of our own homes – and even then damnable, but I don't see how we can escape that one exception.'

Hilaire Belloc writes: 'Certainly in my judgement the plain statement of historical truth is always permissible and often a duty.' Laurence Houseman regards resistance to war as a part of true Christianity: 'Do your Christian friends maintain that children should not be taught religion until they come to full years of discretion?' and mentions that his adopted son aged twenty, thought that if war came he would go and fight and become a conscientious objector afterwards. John Cowper Powys, writing from Dorchester in November 1934, thought that Ellison should certainly go ahead: 'The more anti-war propaganda got out just now all over the world and from every point of view the better.' Not all replied. A note dated 18 November 1934 from Eric Gill says: 'Will reply to yours of Nov. 16 as soon as possible.' He never did and ignored a second letter from Ellison. Dr Albert Schweitzer took over two years to reply. Norman Ellison's letter was only discovered when Dr Schweitzer's English correspondence was being filed!

The most unusual reply he received was from Dr Marie Stopes, a pioneer in birth control, who invited him to join her Society for Constructive Birth Control and Racial Progress and only refers in her letter to the question of birth control in relation to war.

The last two letters received in November 1934 were from Sir James Jeans, known for his work on stellar evolution, and Estelle Sylvia Pankhurst, the suffragette. Norman Ellison ceased letter writing to the famous in the mid-1930s because of the rise of Hitler in Germany and in 1939 the Second World War. There was no need to tell the young what war was like, owing to the arrival of television.

Part 2 includes a selection from the sixty replies Norman Ellison received: Edmund Blunden, Revd P.B. 'Tubby' Clayton, Sir Philip Gibbs, Sir A.P. Herbert, Richard Kearton, A.A. Milne, C.E. Montague, Louis Raemaekers, Erich Maria Remarque, Bertrand Russell, Siegfried Sassoon, Albert Schweitzer, G.B. Shaw, Marie Stopes and Henry Williamson.

EDMUND BLUNDEN (1896–1974)

The poet and writer Edmund Blunden was commissioned in the Royal Sussex Regiment in August 1915, and in the spring of 1916 was posted to the BEF in France. He served for two years in Flanders and the Somme, experiencing Cuinchy Brickstacks and Thiepval Woods. He was awarded the Military Cross in 1917.

Edmund Blunden wrote the following letter dated 7 October 1917 to his sister Phyllis from the Ypres Salient, prior to the final Passchendale battles.

> 'I cannot say what caused it, but I had a terrible dream last night. I was paying out, the orderly Sergeant was shouting out the names, and the men were rolling up for the swag. Suddenly a clap of thunder sounded above, the clouds parted, and a fat angel dressed in a striped football jersey and a bombazine loin cloth gazed down with an eye all bloodshot. In his right hand was a trumpet, in his left hand a roll-call divided into two columns: Sheap and Gotes. Surrounding him were a horde of gorgeous cherubims in pea-green lingerie and holding similar roll-calls and a Venus pencil. The corpulent angel now uplifted his trumpet and puffing his cheeks out like the frog in the fable blew a tremendous blast. Immediately the stars began darting hither and thither and the pay table vanished into space. The company and myself were whirled aloft and immediately placed in the Gotes class. A seraphim with two warts on his left ear now asked us whether we had emergency rations and identity discs. I had not. I was immediately hailed before God. He asked me how long I had been in the Army. I said about forty-five years man and boy. He said "and you come on parade without your iron rations and identity disc? You probably think it's a small offence. Report to the Angel Gabriel's office immediately". I reported, and found the obese party described waiting with a movement order. It read "Menin Road. Front line. For All Eternity".
>
> 'I yelled with terror and awoke to find my batman cleaning my Sunday jacket and the wind howling dreamily between my toes.'

Early in 1918 he was posted from the Somme to a training centre in England, thus being spared the Somme Spring Offensive of the 21 March. Blunden felt a sense of guilt about not being involved in the action: at having survived when so many of his fellow soldiers had died.

After the war he spent some time in journalism. In 1924 he was appointed Professor of English Literature at Tokyo University for three years, and subsequently Fellow and Tutor at Merton College, Oxford (1931–45).

In 1939 at the outbreak of the Second World War he was suspected by some of having Nazi sympathies, mainly as a result of his pacifist views. He returned to the Far East in 1953, having been offered a post at the University of Hong Kong.

In 1918, Blunden had written a full account of his war experiences in *De Bello Germanico, a Fragment of Trench History.* It was not published until 1930, and then only because his brother who wished to set up as a printer was looking for material. 250 copies of this early work were printed.

Whilst in Tokyo and able to distance himself from the events he was describing, he developed *De Bello Germanico* into *Undertones of War* (1928), one of the classic books of the First World War. He was elected Professor of Poetry at Oxford University in 1966. Edmund Blunden was a generous, and modest man. He married three times and had six children.

References

Edmund Blunden, *Undertones of War* Richard Cobden-Sanderson 1928, (Penguin 1982). *Undertones of War* and *De Bello Germanico* (Reissued by the Folio Society, 1989). *The Mind's Eye* (Jonathan Cape, 1934). A collection of essays including 'Flanders', 'Siegfried Sassoon's Poetry', 'Japan', etc.). Barry Webb, *Edmund Blunden. A Biography* (Yale University Press, 1990). *The Poems of Wilfred Owen.* Edited with a memoir and notes by Edmund Blunden. Chatto & Windus 1968 (First published, 1931).

c/o Mr Cobden-Sanderson,
1, Montague Street,
London. W.C. 1.

10th March 1929.

Dear Mr Ellison,

I hope you will not only type out, but also print your exact account of your war, for in spite of all that is extant, war still remains an alluring fantasy to some, or a negligible topic to others. Patriotism is the best power in the world, but it must work by life and not by death, by construction and not destruction. I often find myself in a mood when I could happily rejoin the Royal Sussex at Thiepval – but that's due to despair, and I recover. The question is – Can you obtain the attention of the young generation? I fear not. I should say that my book is read by older people almost entirely. If you can, you'll help England and all her endowments of generous and beautiful action to survive. But suicide is a trait of the English.

Excuse my enforced brevity; thank you for your letter,

Yours sincerely,
Edmund Blunden.

REVD P.B. CLAYTON (1885–1972)

Tubby' Clayton, as he was known, was born in Queensland, Australia. He served as an English Army chaplain during the First World War. In the summer of 1915 he was chaplain to the forces at the hospital at Le Trepport (on the Channel coast north-east of Dieppe). Later he became chaplain to the Buffs and Bedfords in the 16th Infantry Brigade, and was chosen to be the first warden of Toc H in Poperinghe, six miles from Ypres. It was originally named Talbot House in memory of Lt Gilbert Talbot, killed at Ypres in 1915. After the armistice a training scheme for ordination candidates from demobilised soldiers was set up and Clayton was despatched to England to find suitable premises. Owing to the housing shortage, Clayton was told that the only available buildings for his purpose were some redundant gaols. He asked to see one and found himself inspecting Knutsford Gaol in Cheshire. During the war it had been used for conscientious objectors and German prisoners-of-war. It was damp and dilapidated, but Clayton had the imagination to take the opportunity of a home for his ordination candidates, who arrived in March 1919. The ordination school eventually closed in the summer of 1922, although it continued in a somewhat restricted form at 'Kilrie', overlooking Knutsford Heath, until January 1927, when it moved to a new home at Hawarden, Flintshire donated by Henry Gladstone. The Toc H religious and charitable organisation spread throughout the English-speaking world.

References

P.B. Clayton, *Tales of Talbot House* (Chatto & Windus, 1919)
Tresham Lever, *Clayton of Toc H* (J. Murray, 1971)
Will Strachan, *Knutsford Gaol and Tubby Clayton* (Knutsford Historical and Archaeological Association, 1979)

8. 8. 1928.
Alta Gracia.

TOC H
(Once of Poperinghe and Ypres)

South American Tour, 1928.

My dear Ellison,

I've done what you enjoined, and brought your thoughtful letter to the foothills of the Andes. My own poor pinhead view of a view on the tremendous problem of Pacifism such as yours is simply this

1. Any men who weathered 1914–18 or any part of it in the heart of the furnace has a right to his own convictions.

2. Most recent books – even C.E. Montague's which are wonderful – are written by men who only saw the Base – which was base enough to sicken anyone.

3. War is a fearful evil, but not the only one. It is the chastisement of greed, pride, selfishness and hatred. Indulge the passions and war can hardly be avoided. Strike at the root to extirpate it. Don't blame soldiers, but editors, politicians, peoples.

4. Soldiers are like fire-brigades, called in when the flames have caught. Angry nations make war: soldiers make peace! You won't stop fires by refusing to serve in fire-brigades.

5. The so called romance and glory of war is a ghastly sham. But a man can't shelter himself behind others. A Pacifist must prove his sincerity by stretcher-bearing or mine-sweeping. Prisons are safer and more comfortable than trenches.

6. Christ is conquering hate; and when Love wins, there is no defeated party. But He never taught mere softness. He countenanced and even admired the soldierly virtues, cheerfulness, courage, comradeship, sacrifice. War will go like slavery, under the advance of the Kingdom of God ideals throughout the world. A Christian may scruple to defend himself, but I doubt whether he is right to refuse to defend others.

This is all preliminary to the main argument, but it is as much as I can write now. You are I hope in touch with Toc H in Birkenhead or Liverpool. If not please write to my secretary for names and addresses.

All blessings on you and your sons,
Philip Clayton.

SIR PHILIP GIBBS (1877–1962)

Journalist and novelist, he established his considerable reputation as a journalist prior to the War, with the help of such scoops as his exposure of an American explorer (Dr Cook), who claimed to have been to the North Pole, and by his reporting of the disaster of the *Titanic*, enabling the *Chronicle* to put out a special 32-page edition, which sold four million copies.

He achieved a great reputation as a War Correspondent for the *Daily Telegraph* and *Daily Chronicle* during the First World War – the man who dared to tell the truth about Flanders – and was the one correspondent who saw the full horror of the whole four and a half years of the war. He was knighted in 1920, in recognition of his service as journalist and reporter, and was awarded the Chevalier de la Legion d'Honneur.

At the beginning of the First World War, newspaper correspondents who had gone to France without credentials, were liable to be arrested. There were no couriers to take dispatches from France to England. Gibbs writes: 'To get our dispatches home we often had to take them across the Channel, using most desperate endeavours to reach a port of France in time for the next boat home and staying in Fleet Street only for a few hours before hurrying back to Dover or Folkestone in order to plunge again into the fever of invaded France.' He was arrested five times. Eventually early in 1915, on the personal intervention of Lloyd George, who had a connection with the *Chronicle* newspaper, Gibbs was accredited as one of five official war correspondents. However, their reports were vetted by Military censors. Gibbs mentions: 'We lived with our censors and went about with them to dirty places.' One of the censors whom Gibbs had dealings with was C.E. Montague, who later became the deputy editor of the *Manchester Guardian*.

He wrote over ninety books, the last being *Oil*

Lamps and Candle-light (the story of a young family trapped by the Boer War).

References

Philip Gibbs, *The Street of Adventure* (Heinemann, 1909). *The Battles of the Somme* (Heinemann, 1917)

From Bapaume to Passchendaele (Heinemann, 1917). The UK title of *The Struggle in Flanders* (Reprinted by Cedric Chivers Ltd, 1965)

Realities of War (Heinemann, 1920. Reprinted by Cedric Chivers Ltd, 1968)

The Pageant of the Years. Autobiography. (Heinemann, 1946.) *The War Dispatches* (Gibbs and Phillips Ltd, 1964. Edited by Catherine Prigg)

33, Clivedon Place,
S.W.1
Sep. 19th.

Dear Mr Ellison,

Please excuse my delay in answering your very kind letter but I have been away. I was very much pleased and touched by what you wrote, as my memory goes back most vividly to the War days and I feel myself in a kind of spiritual comradeship with all those who went through those times. I well remember my visit to Vaux and my talk with some of the officers and men although I can't bring to mind any one man. It was a curious place and quite unique in its position and way of life. I recollect two sentries in the copse beyond the drawbridge camouflaged in green.

So far I can see nothing good that came out of the war except a wonderful revelation of human endurance. I am desperately afraid that the world has not learnt any lesson from it. The situation in Europe is very disquieting. I have just come back from Germany which is becoming militaristic again, leading of course to increased unrest in France.

I think that you are right to tell your son the plain unvarnished truth. I think we ought to stress the fact that war is unintelligent and that even heroism and all spiritual qualities, are at the mercy of high explosives and the chance of destruction. Man has created agencies which will destroy his civilisation unless they are controlled and mastered by more intelligence and human co-operation than exist at present. I must confess that I am very pessimistic now about the future. The nations seem to be re-grouping themselves for another conflict later on. All the ideals of the League of Nations are being flouted and there is no sign of any slackening of national egotism in favour of closer understanding and goodwill. It is up to us who saw the war, to work for peace.

Kindest regards
Sincerely yours,
Philip Gibbs

SIR A.P. HERBERT (1890–1971)

At the outbreak of war in 1914, he joined the RNVR and was commissioned early in 1915. He was on active service in Gallipoli and in France, with the 63rd Royal Naval Division.

In November 1916, his battalion took part in an attack on Beaucourt – the Somme – in which it was virtually wiped out. A.P. Herbert was one of the officers who survived. A 'failure of morale' during the attack resulted in the court martial and execution of one of the sub-lieutenants. This so distressed A.P. Herbert that on returning to England, after being wounded at the First Battle of Arras in 1917, he began to write his war novel *The Secret Battle*, much of it from personal experience. He completed it 'in a few weeks'. The book concludes with the words, 'My friend Harry was shot for cowardice and he was the bravest man I ever knew.' It is likely that *The Secret Battle* led to reforms in court martial procedure. The book is among the First World War classics and the finest work of literature that A.P. Herbert wrote.

Wounded at the Battle of Arras in 1917, he was invalided back home. Called to the Bar in 1918 he never practised. In 1924 he joined the staff of *Punch*. He was Independent MP for Oxford University, 1939–50, and active in reforming the divorce laws. He was a campaigner for numerous causes, for example, for the Thames Barrage, and for royalties to be paid to authors of books borrowed from public libraries. He wrote novels, verse and musicals enjoying particular success with *Bless the Bride*.

References

A.P. Herbert, *The Secret Battle*. Introduction by Winston S. Churchill. (Methuen, 1919. Hutchinson, 1976)

Reginald Pound, *A.P. Herbert. A Biography* (Michael Joseph, 1976)

12, Hammersmith Terrace,
London. W. 6.

Nov 4th.

Dear Mr Ellison,

Many thanks for your kind and interesting letter. It's difficult to lay down rules for other people, but in principle, I should certainly say that you were right. I think the answer to objectors is that young people, if they are worth anything, will not be made less ready to suffer themselves by hearing the truth, but will think more carefully before they inflict suffering on others.

But then the awful old question arises – 'What is the truth?' And even from the trenches does one see the truth? For example the general view of the activities and value of the Staff seen from the trenches, was by no means the whole truth, as we know.

However, good luck to you. I was with the 63rd (RN) Division – infantry – was 3 months in Gallipoli and 15 months on the Somme, and was then struck (honourably) in the left buttock by a 5.9 at the 1st Battle of Arras.

Yours in haste,
A.P. Herbert.

RICHARD KEARTON (1862–1928)

Naturalist, author and lecturer, born in Thwaite, Upper Swaledale, Yorkshire, where his father was a gamekeeper and farmer. Norman Ellison writes about Richard Kearton in *Over the Hills with Nomad* and describes how during the grouse-shooting season Richard was employed as a loader for Mr Cassell, head of the publishing firm, Cassell & Co. Impressed by the boy Mr Cassell persuaded Richard's father to allow him to come to London to join the publishing firm. He worked for the publishers Cassell and Co. from 1882–1898. Richard Kearton and his brother Cherry were pioneers in the field of wildlife photography, jointly publishing a number of books. They evolved all kinds of weird hiding contrivances such as artificial tree trunks, and dummy sheep and oxen. The photographer was concealed in a hole under the sheep and was literally inside the ox with his camera.

He was a friend of Sir Horace Smith-Dorrien and during the First World War was involved in lecturing to soldiers both fit and wounded.

References

Richard Kearton, *A Naturalist's Pilgrimage* (Cassell, 1926)

Ashdene,
Caterham Valley,
Surrey

9. 3. 27.

Dear Mr Ellison,

A thousand thanks for your kind and interesting letter of the 17th inst.

Pray do not talk about 'taking a liberty' in writing me. When my heart has grown too cold to take an interest in the observations of any fellow student of nature, I shall not be Dicky Kearton and it will be high time it stopped beating.

I have read several personal experiences of men who took part in the Great War and they are a thousand times more interesting to me than all the ponderous compilations of Wobbling Winstons put together. Your ornithological observations agree absolutely with those of my son-in-law, Mr Howard Bentham, who was in the trenches on the Western Front. My brother Cherry had some very interesting and exciting experiences whilst with the Belgian Army and during the fighting in East Africa, but I cannot get him to write about them. The same applies to my eldest son who lived through a rather long experience flying over the Western Front.

A similar disappointment overtakes me when you say that your experiences are to form a strictly family record. Are you influenced by all this tosh about people being sick of hearing about the war? In my humble opinion it is all silly affectation.

You cannot tell what a joy letters like yours are to me now that I am a broken old man. My health gave way just over a year ago and I am now left with a 'groggy' heart and excessive blood pressure. You can imagine what a caterpillar diet, and locomotion restricted to that of a sick snail mean to a man of buoyant spirits and untiring energy. Ah well, I've had an uncommonly good time and am not complaining. It's a great thing to be assured by friends one has never met of help and good healthy pleasures given.

With renewed thanks I remain,
Always faithfully yours,
R. Kearton.

A.A. MILNE (1882–1956)

A.A. Milne was born in 1882 at St John's Wood, London the youngest son of the Headmaster of a private school, Henley House. He was educated at Westminster School and Trinity College, Cambridge where he became editor of the University magazine, *Granta.* In 1906, at the age of twenty-four, he was appointed an Assistant Editor of *Punch.* He held pacifist views prior to the First World War, influenced by Norman Angell's book, *The Great Illusion,* published in 1910. Despite his views he felt on the outbreak of war that he had to do something. As Ann Thwaite comments in her biography 'Milne hoped the war would make people realise the true futility and lunacy of war, and end the sentimentality about it'. He was commissioned in the 11th Royal Warwickshire Regiment in February 1915, and became a Signals Officer, involved in training soldiers on the Isle of Wight.

In July 1916 he was sent on active service to France and served for four months at the Battle of the Somme, being invalided home with Trench fever in November 1916, shortly before the conclusion of the battle. Milne loathed the Army, the filth, the lice, the rats and the lack of any privacy. An amusing example of Army bureaucracy was the occasion when Milne's Commanding Officer received a communication from the Secretary of State for War telling him he would be held personally responsible if any more men arrived in France without toothbrushes!

Milne's pacifist convictions were reinforced by his Somme experiences. In 1934 he published *Peace with Honour. An Enquiry into the War Convention,* which he regarded as his most important book.

A.A. Milne is best known as an author, for the books written for his son Christopher Robin: *When We Were Very Young, Winnie the Pooh, Now We Are Six,* and *The House at Pooh Corner*, published between 1924 and 1928.

The year 1928 marked his meridian. After that came the decline. His last play *Gentlemen Unknown* was a failure. In 1938 when he was 56, Milne wrote *It's Too Late Now* – subtitled *The autobiography of a writer.* As his son Christopher Milne points out, his father wrote his autobiography because it gave him an opportunity to return to his boyhood – a boyhood from which all his inspiration sprang. Half of the autobiography concerns the first 18 years of A.A. Milne's life.

Christopher Milne, who died in April 1996, spent much of his life in retreat from his identification with Christopher Robin. It annoyed him that he was assumed to be the precise model for each child in the books and stories. He wrote one of the first 'spilling the beans on a famous parent' autobiographies, *The Enchanted Places.*

A.A. Milne attacked P.G. Wodehouse in 1941 for his broadcasts on German radio, and accused Wodehouse of refusing the responsibilities of fatherhood. Compton Mackenzie expressed his disgust at this betrayal of a friend at a time when silence was called for (if support was impossible) by writing in a letter to the *Daily Telegraph:* 'I feel more disgusted by Mr Milne's morality than by Mr Wodehouse's irresponsibility.'

Wodehouse achieved a mild revenge on Milne in his novel *The Mating Season,* written in France and published in 1949.

References

A.A. Milne, *It's Too Late Now.* Autobiography (Methuen, 1939 and 1943)

Peace With Honour. An Enquiry into the War Convention (Methuen, 1934 and 1936)

Christopher Milne, *The Enchanted Places* (Eyre Methuen, 1974. Mandarin paperback 1994)

Ann Thwaite, *A.A. Milne. His Life* (Faber and Faber, 1990)

13, Mallord Street,
Chelsea, S.W.3.

30. xi. 29

Dear Sir,

Since you ask for my opinion I will give it. I think it is the duty of any parent to bring his children up with a realisation of the utter futility and wickedness of war. I think that the 'patriotism' which demands the acceptance of war is as admirable as the 'patriotism' which demands the acceptance of unnatural vice. Finally I cannot understand how anybody who thinks as I do can have any hesitation in putting goodness and humour and decency above the feelings of the older members of his family.

Yours faithfully,
A. A. Milne.

C.E. MONTAGUE (1867–1928)

He was forty-seven at the outbreak of war, and a leader writer for the *Manchester Guardian.* He dyed his prematurely white hair, joined the Royal Fusiliers, and by November 1915 was in France. Commissioned in July 1916, he became Censor to the five official war correspondents appointed in early 1915. One of the five correspondents, Sir Philip Gibbs, glimpsed 'some oddity within him, almost a touch of dual personality' and mentions an occasion when they were both watching Germans running out of their dug-outs and being shot as they emerged. Gibbs writes that as they were shot Montague 'laughed in a goblin way'. By way of explaining his laughter which seemed ghoulish to Gibbs he said 'every shell that bursts on the enemy brings the end of the war nearer'. Once he told Gibbs 'that he had declared a kind of moratorium on Christian ethics during the war'. He was mentioned three times in despatches.

Rejoining the staff of the *Manchester Guardian* after the war he eventually became the paper's Assistant Editor.

A most attractive writer his books include *Disenchantment*, a bitter account of his experiences in the First World War. His reply on 7 July 1927 to the letter from Norman Ellison is one of the earliest in the collection.

Reference

C.E. Montague, *Disenchantment* (Chatto and Windus, 1922. Macgibbon, 1968).
Sir P. Gibbs. *Adventures in Journalism.* Chapters 19–20. Heinemann, 1923.
Keith Grieves. 'War Correspondents and Conducting Officers on the Western Front from 1915'. Chapter 51 of *Facing Armageddon* edited by Peter Liddle and Hugh Cecil. Leo Cooper. 1966

Kitts Quarries,
Burford,
Oxon.

March 7/27.

My dear Sir,

I am very sorry that through absence abroad, I have only just received your letter of March 3, on my return.

I sympathise warmly with your feeling and with your wish to make the truth about war known to your sons. In writing about the war as I saw it, a similar wish to protect my own five sons from illusions and suffering was one of my own strongest motives. I shall be most glad if any quotations you care to make from my books, in the manner you describe are of any assistance to you.

Believe me, with best wishes,

Yours sincerely,
C.E. Montague.

LOUIS RAEMAKERS (1869–1956)

A Dutch artist who produced some of the most anti-German war cartoons of the period. His mother was German, his father Dutch. For many years he was a landscape and portrait painter. He turned his attention to political work and became a cartoonist on the staff of the *Amsterdam Telegraaf*, attracting attention throughout Europe. The Germans tried to suppress publication, declaring that 'Raemaekers' cartoons are worth at least two Army Corps to the Allies'. He left neutral Holland to live in England. His wife received anonymous postcards warning her that his ship would certainly be torpedoed in the North Sea. France awarded him the Cross of the Legion of Honour.

Reference

Raemaekers Cartoons (Land and Water edition. Edited by Francis Stopford, 1916)

Bruxelles,
7, Avenue De L'Hippodrome,
Tel. 30619

March 11th, 1927.

Dear Sir,

Please excuse my not answering earlier your letter of Feb 28th. I am very irregular in my correspondence, I'm sorry to say, and only now and again I find time enough to look after it.

I subscribe entirely to what you wrote about the stupid brutality of warfare imposed on peaceful peoples. Since I have seen war at work in France and Belgium I think it my duty to do everything I can to prevent a new war with still greater horrors.

Anything which you can do to make your country-men understand, that France and Belgium are, more than any other countries in the whole world, anxious to have no more war, and that they will go to the very limit which is compatible with their security as independent states, will be a fair and honest service tendered to them and to the rest of Europe.

It is because I have realised that some people in England and America have been brought to believe stories about French (and Belgian) militarism and imperialism, that I speak to you about this, seeing from your letter how well inspired you are. For I feel that you too, when you know a little about the real nature and mind of these most exposed peoples, you must understand how cruel and unjust such accusations are.

Thanking you for your kind letter,
Yours faithfully,
Louis Raemaekers.

ERICH MARIA REMARQUE (1898–1970)

Born in Osnabrück, Germany his family was of French extraction, having emigrated into Germany at the time of the French Revolution. In November 1916, at the age of eighteen, he was sent to the Western Front. On 31 July 1917 during the Battle of Passchendaele he was hit by shrapnel and spent some time in hospital in Duisberg. In September 1917 his mother died. It came as a great blow to him, shortly to be followed by the early death of his great friend Fritz Horstemeier.

Remarque had a succession of jobs: an organist in an asylum, a music teacher, motor car dealer and, eventually after a time abroad, a motor specialist in Berlin. In January 1929 he published *All Quiet on the Western Front* or *Im Westen nichts Neues,* a graphic account of the horrors of war, and the most famous anti-war novel of the period. By the end of 1929, it had sold a million copies in Germany alone. Translated into English in March 1929, it led to an interesting exchange of letters between Remarque and General Sir Ian Hamilton, who after the war conducted a campaign against the Versailles settlement. He saw the book as the story of how the terrible demands of attritional warfare had produced a 'lost' generation. He urged Remarque to write another book exposing the enormity of modern war.

In an interview in 1929, Remarque gives his reasons for writing the novel. He says that in trying to understand why he suffered from serious periods of depression he eventually found his way back to his war experiences: 'I could observe a similar phenomenon in many of my friends and acquaintances. The shadow of the war hung over us, especially when we tried to shut our minds to it. The very day this thought struck me, I put pen to paper, without much in the way of prior thought.' He goes on to say that he was seeking to do no more than to write a 'worm's eye view' of the war. In 1930 *All Quiet on the Western Front* was made into one of the first talking films at Universal studios in Hollywood. It won two Oscars and was the first great anti-war film.

Remarque wrote a sequel *The Road Back* (*Der Weg Zunick*), published in 1931.

When the Nazis came to power Remarque left Germany to live in Switzerland. His refusal to return to Germany resulted in his being stripped of his German citizenship by Hitler and the burning of his books. Remarque emigrated to America. From 1939–42 he spent most of his time in Hollywood. He had a close friendship with Marlene Dietrich. His other friends included Greta Garbo, Charlie Chaplin, Cole Porter, and the writers Ernest Hemingway and F. Scott Fitzgerald. In 1947, he became an American citizen and eleven years later married the film star Paulette Goddard, his second wife.

Remarque died in Locarno, Switzerland, on 25 September 1970 at the age of 72. The manuscript of *All Quiet on the Western Front*, was, following his death, in the possession of his first wife. In October 1995 it was sent for auction at Sotheby's of London. The manuscript was sold for a quarter of a million pounds to Erich Remarque's home town of Osnabrück.

References

C.R. Barker and R.W. Last, *Erich Maria Remarque* (Oswald Wolff and Harper & Row, 1979)

E. Maria Remarque, *All Quiet On The Western Front* (G. P. Putnam's Sons. 1929. Cape 1994)

The Road Back. (G. P. Putnam's Sons. 1931. Mayflower 1979)

Berlin, den 15. Juli 1929

Sehr geehrter Herr Ellison!

Ich danke Ihnen für Ihren freundlichen Brief und die Anerkennung meines Buches! Wenn Sie selbst ein Tagebuch schreiben und glauben, dass Sie den Erlebnissen, die Sie gehabt haben, so objektiv wie es moglich ist, gegenuberstehen konnen, so wird es sicherlich, ob es nun veroffentlicht wird oder nicht, im kleineren oder im grosseren Freise zum Fortschritt beitragen, und der Fortschritt-das wird sech wohl heute jeder einsichtige Mensch glauben-liegt im Frieden und im Wunsch nach Frieden!

Ich grusse Sie herzlich als,
Ihr ergebenster,
E. Maria Remarque.

Translation

Berlin.

15th July, 1929.

Dear Mr Ellison,

I thank you for your friendly letter and the appreciation of my book. If you write a diary of your War experiences with the intention of making these as striking and objective as possible, it is obvious even if it is published now or not, that the work will assist either more or less materially in universal progress, and every far-seeing person will believe that this progress will be achieved by peace or the will for peace.

I greet you most sincerely as,
E. Maria Remarque.

BERTRAND RUSSELL (1872–1970)

With both parents dead by the time he was four, Bertrand Russell grew up as an only child in a house dominated by his grandmother. In his early twenties he became a fellow of Trinity College, Cambridge. He produced work of lasting importance in the fields of philosophy and mathematical logic. By the time of the First World War, Russell was a champion of women's suffrage, was against conscription and in favour of a negotiated peace.

He pursued his vigorous anti-war campaign. In 1915 he joined the No Conscription Fellowship and later became involved in a court case regarding a young St Helens schoolmaster, Ernest Everett, who was granted exemption from military service. The court, however, went out of their way to recommend his dismissal from school, and recognised his conscientious claim only so far as to award him non-combatant service – which he ignored. He was sentenced to two years hard labour at a court martial on 10 April 1916. Russell drew up a leaflet outlining the case. 'Two years' hard labour for refusing to obey the dictates of conscience'. It embarrassed the authorities who thought that the leaflet would hamper recruiting. On 5 June 1916, Russell was brought to trial at the Mansion House in London. He was found guilty and fined one hundred pounds or 61 days in prison. His appeal was rejected and because he refused to pay the fine there was a forced sale of some of his belongings. He was described by the Foreign Office as 'one of the most mischievous cranks in the country'. As a result of his activities he was relieved of his Fellowship at Trinity College, Cambridge in July 1916. However, he continued his opposition, publishing *Principles of Social Reconstruction* (1916) in which he defined the role of the pacifist and analysed war as a social phenomenon. In February 1918 he was sentenced to six months in prison for advocating in public that the British Government accept a German offer to open peace negotiations.

He once likened himself to a fish in an aquarium, trying to make contact but unable to communicate. All he could ever see in the glass was his own reflection. Bertrand Russell was awarded the Order of Merit and the Nobel Prize for Literature in 1950. He was married four times and from 1955 lived at Plas Penryhn on the Portmeirion peninsula, N. Wales until his death at the age of 97 in 1970.

References

The Autobiography of Bertrand Russell. Three volumes: Volume 1, (1872–1914); Volume 2, (1914–1944); Volume 3 (1944–1967) (Allen & Unwin Ltd, 1967, 1968 and 1969)

Ronald W. Clark, *The Life of Bertrand Russell* (J. Cape & Weidenfeld and Nicolson, 1975. Penguin Books Ltd, 1978)

Ray Monk, *Bertrand Russell: The Spirit of Solitude* (Cape, 1996)

B. Russell, *Portraits From Memory and other Essays* (includes 'Experiences of a Pacifist in the First World War') (Allen & Unwin Ltd, 1956)

The letter to Norman Ellison from Bertrand Russell is from Beacon Hill on the Sussex Downs, a progressive school that Russell founded with his second wife Dora.

BEACON HILL SCHOOL

Harting,
Petersfield.

Telephone & Telegrams
Harting 6.
Principal at Home: Wednesdays 2.30–5.

19th December 1928.

Dear Sir,

In reply to your letter of the 14th December, my own view would be that you are doing absolutely the right thing. You say that the older members of your family consider that to tell children the truth is to 'prejudice young minds before they are old enough to judge for themselves'. I gather that the older members of your family, like the bulk of mankind, consider that to tell children lies is not to prejudice their young minds, for no-one can deny that the ordinary teaching of schools, of parsons, and of elderly persons on the subject of war consists of lies from beginning to end.

My own view, upon which I act with my own children, is that no fact of any sort or kind should be concealed from the young if their curiosity leads them to wish to know about it. I know some pacifists, for example, who try to prevent children for as long as possible from knowing that wars occur; but this seems to me quite as pernicious as the militarist teaching that wars are a kind of picnic. The essence of sanity and of true morality is to be able to live in the world as it is without the support of fairy tales. I should therefore be whole-heartedly with you in what you are planning to do.

Yours faithfully,
Bertrand Russell.

SIEGFRIED SASSOON (1886–1967)

The Sassoons, an extraordinary Jewish dynasty, were known as 'the Rothschilds of the East' due to their spectacular banking and trading empire based on Bombay with branches in the Far East and Europe. The founder of the family fortune was David Sassoon. He sent one of his sons, S.D. Sassoon, to England in 1858 to open an English branch of the company. S.D. Sassoon had a daughter and two sons, one of whom, Alfred, was Siegfried Sassoon's father.

Siegfried Sassoon was born in Kent and brought up by his mother after his father Alfred left her when Siegfried was five. He was educated at Marlborough and Cambridge but left without taking a degree.

Enlisting in August 1914 as a trooper in the Sussex Yeomanry he was commissioned in December 1914 in the First Battalion of the Royal Welch Fusiliers. In December 1915 Sassoon joined 'C' Company of the First Battalion and met fellow officer Robert Graves. He describes Graves in his diary as an 'interesting creature, overstrung and self-conscious, a defier of convention'. Sassoon fought at Mametz Wood in the Somme offensive of July 1916 and was awarded the Military Cross. In August 1916, due to illness, he was sent back to England. He returned to France in February 1917 but wounded in April 1917, was invalided back home in June. He visited the pacifist Bertrand Russell and decided to make a public statement, explaining what the war was really like. (The meeting is described, thinly disguised, in *Memoirs of an Infantry Officer.)* The statement began: 'I am making this statement as an act of wilful defiance of military authority.' He thought it morally wrong that the war should be prolonged and circulated the statement to leading politicians and journalists. This had no immediate effect, so Sassoon sent a copy of his statement to his Commanding Officer accompanied by a letter stating: 'It is my intention to refuse to perform any further military duties as a protest against the policy of the Government in prolonging the war by failing to state their conditions of peace.' Fellow officer Robert Graves was horrified. He agreed with the views expressed, but thought that Sassoon was acting in a disloyal manner. Graves managed to arrange that Sassoon was brought before a medical board instead of a court martial on the grounds that he was ill. The board decided that Sassoon was not responsible for his actions and sent him to Craiglockhart Hospital in Scotland, for 'shell-shocked' soldiers. The efforts of Robert Graves to hush up Sassoon's 'defiance letter' failed, the open letter from Sassoon to his C.O. being published in *The Times* on 31 July 1917.

Sassoon wrote some of his bitterest war poems whilst at Craiglockhart hospital. He met Wilfred Owen whose works he helped to publish after Owen was killed at the Front on 4 November, 1918. After 3 months in hospital Sassoon returned to active service in Palestine and then France. He was wounded again on 13 July 1918, by mistake, by one of his own NCOs, as he returned from a dawn patrol.

After the war he returned to his life of country gentleman, but, as he wrote in 1920, wished that he could 'find a moral equivalent for war'. Unable to find it he was a slightly bewildered figure writing in his volumes of autobiography of the world he had lost. He became a Roman Catholic in 1957.

It was his anti-war poetry and his public affirmation of pacifism after he had won the Military Cross and was still in the army that made him widely known. Robert Graves in *Goodbye To All That* says of Sassoon 'He varied between happy warrior and bitter pacifist.'

Sassoon wrote a semi-fictitious autobiography, *The Complete Memoirs of George Sherston*, which includes The Memoirs of a Fox-Hunting Man, The Memoirs of an Infantry Officer and Sherston's Progress.

Hamo Sassoon (Siegfried's brother), who had hurried back from the Argentine to enlist with the

Royal Engineers, was hit by a sniper's bullet at Gallipoli in 1915, and died after having his leg amputated. Siegfried's millionaire cousin, Sir Philip Sassoon, was private secretary to Field Marshal Haig and to Lloyd George.

References

Dominic Hibberd, *Wilfred Owen. The Last Year 1917–1918.* (Constable & Co, 1992)
Stanley Jackson, *The Sassoons. Portrait of a Dynasty* (Heinemann, 1968 and 1989)
Siegfried Sassoon, *Diaries '1915–1918'*, ed. R. Hart-Davis (Faber and Faber, 1983)
The War Poems, ed. R. Hart Davis (Faber and Faber, 1983)
The Memoirs of an Infantry Officer (Faber and Faber, 1930 and 1965)
Martin Taylor, *Two Fusiliers: the First World War friendship of Robert Graves and S. Sassoon*, review no 7. (The Imperial War Museum, 1992)

23, Campden Hill Square,
London W.8.

8. 12. 29.

Dear Mr Ellison,

I am very glad that my book has given you satisfaction. All the war experience described is of course strictly accurate, and you can find more if you want it in my numerous war poems written between 1915 and 1919.

If you can provide your sons with an exact account of your war experience, you will be doing them a good service. If they prefer to take 'patriotic' opinions of the generation who were not at the war front – so much the worse for them! As you say no one really knows about the war except the infantry (and artillery). Have you read ***Undertones of War*** *by E. Blunden? A very sound book, and beautifully written, by a man who always tells the truth. If you care to send me your typewritten diary, I should read it with deep interest.*

With all good wishes,
Yours very truly,
Siegfried Sassoon.

I played cricket for my reserve battalion (3rd RW Fus), against a Wallasey XI in 1915, and made 58 (out of a total of 120), a fact which still gives me great pleasure.

ALBERT SCHWEITZER (1875–1965)

Born in Alsace, France, he achieved worldwide fame as a musician, theologian, and medical missionary. An organist and authority on J.S. Bach, he studied medicine and in 1913 went to Lambarene in (what was then) French Equatorial Africa where he established a mission hospital. He received the Nobel Prize for Peace in 1953.

References
Albert Schweitzer, *On the Edge of the Primeval Forest* (A & C. Black, 1922. First English edition)
More From the Primeval Forest (A. & C. Black, 1931)
My Life and Thought (Allen and Unwin 1933. Second edition Guild Books, 1955)

From Mrs L.E.B. Russell,
Hospital du Dr A. Schweitzer,
Lambarene,
Afrique Equatoriale Francaise
via Bordeaux-Port Gentil.

22. 9. 30.

Dear Sir,

Dr Schweitzer has asked me to write and express to you his deep regret and apologies that your letter of May 1928 received no answer. I am engaged in filing his English letters of the last four years, and he is shocked at my discovery of your letter among those not answered.

Madame Schweitzer, when with him, undertakes his English correspondence, as he does not write our language himself. But she suffers frequent attacks of ill health, and when these occur when she is with the Doctor on his concert and lecture tours, she is forced to postpone replies to all but the most urgent communications. This must be the explanation of your failure to receive an answer.

Dr Schweitzer is glad to know you enjoyed his broadcast organ recital. I enjoyed it still more for I was with him at the Bishopsgate Institute! No doubt you know now his three beautiful HMV gramophone records? And he is pleased that you were so interested in 'The Quest of the Historical Jesus'. He returned here at Christmas very weary after writing his great new book **The Mysticism of St Paul** *– at the same time he was travelling in many countries to raise money to carry on and develop this Hospital, by organ recitals and lectures. The St Paul will shortly appear in English, as will the second volume of* **On the Edge of the Primeval Forest**, *and a little later the Autobiography on which he is now at work when his day's work is ended – for he is actively engaged all day, not only as doctor, but as builder, land developer, etc. I think in these books and especially, if you do not already know them, in the two volumes (out of four) already published of his Philosophy of Civilization – viz* **The Decay and Restoration of Civilization and Civilization and Ethics**, *you will find help in seeking the answers to many questions.*

I am leaving next week after a second stay of twenty months. If you should ever wish for any information about Dr Schweitzer's movements, etc, address me at the Overseas League, Park Place, St James's Street, London, S.W.1.

With Dr Schweitzer's kind regards,
Yours faithfully,
L. M. Russell.

Translation of note in French from Dr Schweitzer

Dear Sir,

Teach your son the truth: that war is stupid, atrocious and useless! We all want to march towards the future, where war will only be a memory of the past! With my kind regards,

Yours very sincerely,
Albert Schweitzer.

GEORGE BERNARD SHAW (1856–1950)

Born in Dublin, he moved to London in 1876 to begin his journalistic career as a music critic. Few were as perceptive as Shaw in recognising the genius of Wagner. He was also an influential champion of British composers.

Author of over fifty plays, many contained prefaces in which Shaw expresses his views as a champion of the thinking man. He was a freethinker, supporter of women's rights, and a member of the Fabian Society.

In his book *Commensense about the War* (1914), Shaw criticised the muddle of British Foreign policy before 1918. He received an invitation from Sir Douglas Haig to visit the Western Front and was advised to wear khaki tunic and breeches, and a pair of trench boots for the yellow Flanders mud, but his camouflage was defeated by a mantle of brilliant snow covering the battlefield.

Shaw was introduced to Sir Philip Gibbs who remembers going to lunch with one of the Generals who hated having Shaw as guest. Courtesy, however, overcame his ill-temper and he turned to Shaw, who was having a lively conversation with his ADCs, and asked a polite question: 'Well Mr Shaw when do you think this War will be over?' 'Well General,' said Shaw, 'We are all anxious for an early and dishonourable peace.' This reduced the General to silence for quite a time, but the ADCs set up a howl of mirth. Upon his return to England, Shaw wrote a series of articles about his experiences in the War zone which maddened his critics even by the title, which was *Joy Riding at the Front*. One MP reminded the House of Commons that GBS had advised British soldiers to shoot their officers and go home, and demanded if this was the sort of man who should be officially invited to visit the Front.

He was awarded the Nobel Prize in 1925. Shaw was a prolific letter writer (for example, his correspondence with Ellen Terry and Mrs Patrick

Campbell), a strict vegetarian and never drank spirits, coffee or tea. He died at the age of 94.

References

Michael Holroyd, *The Pursuit of Power* (1898–1918), volume 2 of his biography of Shaw (Chatto & Windus, 1989. Penguin, 1993)

G.B. Shaw, *What I Really Wrote About the War* (Constable, 1930)

10, Adelphi Terrace, W.C.2.

10th March 1927.

Dear Sir

Mr Bernard Shaw desires me to say that all books must justify themselves by their quality; but anyone who produces a genuine record of the war is doing a public service. If his father had been through a war he would certainly want to know what it was like, and greatly resent being told lies about it.

Yours faithfully,
Blanche Patch,
Secretary.

MARIE STOPES (1880–1958)

Marie Stopes was a pioneer in the field of birth control. A lecturer in Fossil Botany at Manchester University, she published *The Study of Plant Life for Young People* in 1906 and *Ancient Plants* in 1910.

She had an unfulfilled personal life. *Married Love,* written in 1916 whilst still a virgin, advised separate bedrooms for married couples. The failure of her first marriage, annulled because it was unconsummated, turned her attention to marital unhappiness caused by ignorance regarding contraception. Her second marriage in 1918 was to the aircraft manufacturer, Humphrey V. Roe. Their son was born in March, 1924. Eventually the marriage deteriorated and in July 1938 she exacted statements from her husband permitting her sexual carte blanche. He was banished to a wing of their house.

Marie Stopes advocated selective breeding in order to improve the human race (eugenics). In the 1920s she wanted her birth control clinics to 'provide a sure light in our racial darkness'. Mothers attending her clinics who were either physically or mentally defective were advised to be sterilised. She interfered in the marriage of her son to the gifted daughter of Barnes Wallis (inventor of the bouncing bomb), on the grounds that his future wife was short-sighted, a defect which she claimed

TEL. MUSEUM 9528.

C.B.C.

THE SOCIETY FOR

Constructive Birth Control and Racial Progress.

President:
MARIE CARMICHAEL STOPES, D.Sc., Ph.D., F.L.S., F.G.S.

Vice-Presidents:

COUNCILLOR MARGARET ASHTON, M.A.
SIR JAMES BARR, C.B.E., M.D., F.R.S.Ed.
COL. R. J. BLACKHAM, C.B., D.S.O., M.D.
EDWARD CARPENTER, ESQ.
PROFESSOR A. M. CARR-SAUNDERS, M.A.
THE HON. SIR JOHN COCKBURN, K.C.M.G., M.D.
THE REV. H. G. CORNER, D.D.
VISCOUNTESS GREY OF FALLODEN.

SIR ANTHONY HOPE HAWKINS, M.A.
JULIAN S. HUXLEY, M.A.
PROFESSOR DAVID STARR JORDAN, M.S., PH.D., M.D., LL.D.
J. M. KEYNES, M.A., C.B.
COUNCILLOR E. KING, J.P. (Ex-Mayor of Islington).
SIR GEORGE H. KNIBBS, C.M.G., F.R.A.S.
SIR W. ARBUTHNOT LANE, BART., C.B., M.B.

MRS. PETHICK LAWRENCE.
SIR DAVID MURRAY, R.A.
THE LADY OSSULSTON.
SIR ARCHDALL REID, M.B., F.R.S.Ed.
RT. HON. G. H. ROBERTS, P.C., J.P.
MRS. ALEC TWEEDIE, F.R.G.S.
PROFESSOR E. A. WESTERMARCK, PH.D.
J. HAVELOCK WILSON, ESQ., C.H., C.B.E.

Hon. Secretary: COUNCILLOR H. V. ROE. *Hon. Treasurer:* COL R. J. BLACKHAM, C.B., C.M.G., D.S.O., M.D.

Hon. Solicitors: MESSRS. BRABY & WALLER, Dacre House, Arundel Street, Strand.

Auditor: MISS M. M. HOMERSHAM, M.A., A.S.A.A., 106, St. Clement's House, E.C. 4.

Bankers: MIDLAND BANK LIMITED, 159 & 160, Tottenham Court Road, W. 1.

General Executive Committee:

A. S. E. ACKERMANN, B.Sc.(Eng.), F.C.G.I.
LADY DUCKHAM.
MRS. ENID EVE.
ALFRED GOODMAN, ESQ.

AUSTIN HARRISON, ESQ.
REV. LEWIS JEFFERSON.
LADY LANE.
AYLMER MAUDE, ESQ.

W. P. PYCRAFT, F.Z.S., F.L.S.
EARL RUSSELL.
MRS. STANLEY WRENCH.

OFFICIAL ORGAN—
Birth Control News.

108, WHITFIELD STREET,
TOTTENHAM COURT ROAD,
LONDON, W.1.

9th May, 1927.

Dear Sir

Thank you for your letter of the 4th inst. The question of birth control in relation to war has always been in my mind and I frequently refer to it in lectures and other ways. I have frequently advocated a League of Nations prepared to keep their birth rate within their own bounds. You will see in particular the exposure we give of Mussolini in the **Birth Control News** *enclosed.*

I sincerely hope as you are interested in these matters you will join the Society of which I have pleasure in enclosing membership form and copy of the tenets herewith.

Yours faithfully,
M. C. Stopes.

threatened to impair the purity of her grandchildren. She refused to attend the wedding, and on her death in 1958, she bequeathed her eighteenth century mansion, Norbury Park in Surrey, to the Royal Society of Literature, and the *Greater Oxford Dictionary* in 13 volumes to her son.

Marie Stopes made married life happier for many other women despite the failure of her own marriages. In her reply to Norman Ellison's letter she ignored his request for advice about publishing his War Diary, inviting him instead to join her Society for Constructive Birth Control and Racial Progress.

References

Marie Stopes, *Married Love* (Originally published in 1918. Republished Gollancz, 1995)

Harry Verdon Stopes-Roe and Ian Scott, *Marie Stopes and Birth Control* (Priory, 1974)

June Rose, *Marie Stopes and the Sexual Revolution* (Faber & Faber, 1992)

HENRY WILLIAMSON (1895–1977)

Enlisted in the London Rifle Brigade, Henry Williamson crossed to France in November 1914. A letter to his mother, subsequently published in the *Daily Express*, described the famous 1914 Christmas truce and fraternization with German troops, an event that made a lasting personal impression. As Anne Williamson comments in her biography of Henry Williamson 'he saw that war was created by greed, misplaced zeal and bigotry. He could never forget that the German soldiers thought as deeply and sincerely as the English that they were fighting for God and Country'.

Commissioned in May 1915 he became a Transport Officer with the Machine-Gun Corps. For three months (March to May 1917), Williamson was involved in the attack on the Hindenburg Line, and for three weeks in 1918, the German Spring Offensive. The First World War was a crucial period in Henry Williamson's life and influenced much of his writing.

After the War he turned to farming in Norfolk, moving to Georgeham in North Devon in 1921. In 1925 part of his honeymoon with his first wife, Loetitia, was spent revisiting the battlefields of the First World War. *The Wet Flanders Plain* was published in 1929. He wrote more than fifty books the best known being *Tarka the Otter*, first privately printed and published by the author in an edition limited to one hundred copies in August, 1927. It has since become a classic. This book along with *Salar the Salmon* (1935) was illustrated by the Macclesfield-born artist, Charles Tunnicliffe, who also illustrated all of the *Nomad* books by Norman Ellison. The gradual deterioration in their friendship is described by Ian Niall in *Portrait of a Country Artist*, and throws light on the temperament of a sensitive and gifted writer. He spent the Second World War as a farmer in Norfolk, returning to North Devon in 1959 to a cottage in Capstone Place, Ilfracombe, North Devon, where he lived with his second wife, Christine.

Apart from his nature writing Williamson published between 1951 and 1961 a fifteen volume autobiographical novel sequence, *A Chronicle of Ancient Sunlight,* described by the military historian and diarist, Alan Clark as 'still far the best illustration of history as fiction I have ever encountered'.

There is no doubt that Henry Williamson was a difficult and complicated man. He was not an intellectual. He was politically naive and his support for Hitler and Sir Oswald Mosley damaged his reputation. He was also intolerant and rather arrogant. Very observant, he was not an expert naturalist. He had, however, an unusual affinity with animals, and an ability to convey the atmosphere and beauty of the Devon countryside, clearly illustrated in *Tarka the Otter.* Williamson's last books were *A Clear Water Stream* (1958), *The Gale of the World* (1969), and *The Scandaroon* (1972). He wrote the foreword to the 1973 facsimile edition of *The Wipers Times*, first produced in a rat-infested cellar in Ypres in February 1916 and never printed out of the Front area until the final number in December 1918.

References

Daniel Farson, *Henry Williamson. A Portrait.* (Michael Joseph. 1982)

Ian Niall, *Portrait of a Country Artist. Charles Tunnicliffe. R.A.* (Gollancz, 1980)

Anne Williamson, *Tarka and the Last Romantic* (Alan Sutton, 1995)

Henry Williamson, *The Wet Flanders Plain* (Beaumont Press, 1929. Faber, 1929. Gliddon Books Pbk. 1987).

Henry Williamson *The Patriot's Progress* (Geoffrey Bles, 1930. Macdonald 1968.)

The Wipers Times 1973 Facsimile edition with foreword by Henry Williamson. Introduction, notes and glossary by Patrick Beaver. Published by Peter Davies.

Skirr Cottage,
Georgeham,
North Devon.

29th June, 1929.

Dear Sir,

The truth lasts, especially the truth stated without comment, without a propaganda intent. But comment may be inspired and we get great poetry, but genius is very rare.

We ordinary folk (I am presumptuous, for you may be a great poet), must content ourselves with writing just what happened.

If you would care to send me your diary when typed, I would willingly give you an opinion on it. Above all listen only to your own heart – not even to me.

Yours faithfully,
Henry Williamson.

P.S. Books of the sort you describe are by no means the exception. Get ***Under Fire*** *in the Everyman edition, and* ***A Subaltern on the Somme.*** *Also a new book out soon* ***Combed Out*** *(Cape).*

PART THREE

BACKGROUND INFORMATION

1
WESTERN FRONT CHRONOLOGY

1914

3 August. France and Germany declare war on each other. 4 August. Germany declares war on Belgium and immediately crosses her frontier. Britain and Belgium declare war on Germany.

1. ***Battle of LIEGE***, 5–16 August. Liege was the main stronghold of Belgian defences. German troops crossed the frontier into Belgium on 4 August, intending to march on Paris. Troops were in possession of the town and citadel by 7 August but the surrounding forts did not succumb until the Germans brought 42 cm heavy howitzers (siege guns) into action against them on 12 August. The last of the Liege forts fell on 16 August. The Belgians then withdrew to Antwerp.
2. ***Battle of MONS***, 23–24 August. First serious battle on the Western Front involving the British. Resulted in heavy casualties (1,600 killed or wounded) and lost ground. The BEF retreated south from Mons towards the French frontier.
3. ***Battle of LE CATEAU***, 26 August. The British inflicted heavy losses on the superior German force before resuming its retreat, a most successful delaying tactic by General Smith-Dorrien. The intended withdrawal by Sir J. French of the BEF from supporting the French Army was prevented by the intervention of Lord Kitchener, Secretary of State for War (1 September).
4. ***Battle of the MARNE***, 5–9 September. The westwards German advance to Paris was halted by the British and the French. A decisive battle which cost both sides heavy casualties, but ended all hopes of a quick victory by the Germans.
5. ***First Battle of the AISNE***, 13–14 September.
6. ***Siege and Fall of ANTWERP***, 28 September–9 October.
7. ***First Battle of YPRES***, 14 October–22 November. Resulted in stalemate and established the Western Front and trench warfare.
8. The Unofficial Christmas Day Truce. Fraternisation between the Germans and their enemies took place almost everywhere in the British No-Man's Land.

At the end of 1914 Germany held the strategic advantage occupying nearly all of Belgium (except for the area near Ypres), as well as a large area of Northern France.

1915

The failure of BEF operations in 1915 was due in part to Britain being the junior partner to France, committed to removing the Germans from French territory. General Joffre (France) was for all practical purposes the Commander-in-Chief. Sir John French was in command of the BEF, with Sir Douglas Haig in charge of the British First Army and Sir Horace Smith-Dorrien in charge of the British Second Army.

1. ***Battle of NEUVE CHAPELLE***, 10–13 March. The first British offensive of the war. Although a carefully prepared offensive by Haig it was not entirely successful due to inaccurate artillery fire and a five-hour delay in launching the infantry assault. There were heavy casualties.
2. ***Capture and Defence of HILL 60***, (Ypres) 17 April–21 April.
3. ***Second Battle of YPRES***, 22 April–25 May. The first chorine gas attack by the Germans on the 22 April in the Langemarck–St Julien area in the north-east of the Salient. Further offensives using gas took place to the end of April and into May.

Canadian troops played a vital role both in defence and attack. Sir John French dismissed the Commander of the Second Army, Sir Horace Smith-Dorrien appointing General Sir W. Plumer in his place (see page 52).

4. ***Battle of AUBERS RIDGE***, 9 May. The British contribution to this Allied offensive was abandoned after one day owing to the loss of 12,000 men. A shortage of heavy guns and high explosive shells allowed the German positions to escape destruction and heavy fire to be directed on advancing British troops. Sir John French gave detailed information about the shell shortage to the war correspondent of *The Times*, Colonel Charles Repington. His first dispatch was published on 14 May. The so-called 'shell scandal' resulted in Lloyd George being given responsibility for a Ministry of Munitions, and in Asquith having to form a coalition government on 26 May.

5. ***Battle of Festubert*** (15–27 May). 18 July. The British Third Army formed under the command of Field Marshal Allenby.

6. Heavy fighting at ***HOOGE (Ypres Salient)***, 29–31 July. Flamethrowers were used against the British by the Germans.

7. ***Battle of LOOS***, September. The British used chlorine gas for the first time near Loos, a small mining village, just north of Lens. The effective use of machine-guns by the Germans resulted in a terrible slaughter of the British infantry. Initial success turned to failure due to the reserves not being available in time, being kept miles to the rear. Of 10,000 British soldiers, 385 officers and 7,861 men were killed or wounded.

The Commander-in-Chief, Sir John French was sent home in December 1915 (as a result of his lack of judgement at Ypres and Loos), and replaced by Sir Douglas Haig.

Chantilly Conference, December 1915. A War Council Meeting of the Allies – Britain, France, Russia, and Italy – that determined to regain the military initiative the following year. It was not until 14 February that Haig agreed to accept the plan of Marshal Joffre for a 1 July assault. The British/French plan was for a massive joint attack of equal strength, in the Somme region at the junction of the two armies, in order to break through the German lines. However, the major role fell to the British due to the events at Verdun in late February, leaving the French with insufficient troops to make a major contribution to the Somme offensive.

1916

On the 3 February the British Military Service Act came into force replacing voluntary enlistment with compulsory military service.

1. On the 21 February the Germans launched a massive attack against the French at ***VERDUN,*** defended by two principal fortresses, Fort Vaux and Fort Douaumont. The battle continued for ten months (21 February–15 December 1916) – the longest battle of the war. There were extremely heavy casualties on both sides. The Germans captured Fort Douaumont on 25 February. Fort Vaux, after holding out for three months, fell to the Germans on 7 June, but was recaptured by the French on 3 November. On 15 December the French launched a massive offensive pushing back the German line to its position the previous March.

Alistair Horne, author of *The Price of Glory. Verdun 1916*, comments: 'Neither side "won" at Verdun. It was the indecisive battle in an indecisive war; the battle that had no victors in a war that had no victors.'

On 1 March the British Fourth Army was formed under the command of General Rawlinson.

Death at sea of Field Marshal Kitchener on 5 June. His ship struck a mine en route to Russia.

2. ***First Battle of the SOMME***, a series of battles 1 July–18 November. Launched jointly with the French to relieve pressure on the French army defending Verdun. The front ran NW–SE, 6 km east of Albert across the valley of the Ancre over the almost treeless high ground north of the Somme, now hedgeless wheat fields.

Rawlinson's Fourth Army were to conduct the main assault on a fourteen mile front, north of the Somme between Maricourt and Serre. The infantry bombardment commenced on 24 June, but the attack intended for 29 June was postponed until 1 July owing to the bad weather. The 1st July 1916 was a day marked by probably the greatest single catastrophe of the whole war. At 7 a.m. the bombardment was at its height. Nearly quarter of a million shells were fired in an hour, and at 7.28 a.m. ten mines were exploded under German trenches. At 7.30 a.m. eleven British divisions advanced simultaneously. As the infantry moved forwards the German machine-guns opened fire. Two German-held villages, Mametz and Montauban were captured. The toll on British troops during the first day of the Somme offensive was higher than on any other single day of the war. Over a thousand British officers and more than 20,000 men were killed with 25,000 seriously wounded. Complete battalions such as The Sheffield Pals and The Accrington Pals suffered enormous losses. In July the actions included Fricourt, Trones Wood, Mametz Woods and Delville Wood. Anzac troops were involved in the attack on Pozieres. Liddell Hart quotes one of the most level-headed officers in the force writing: 'We have just come out of a place so terrible that . . . a raving lunatic, could never imagine the horror of the last thirteen days.'

On the 30 July at Guillemont 500 men of three Liverpool Pals battalions were killed. The villages of Guillemont and Ginchy were eventually captured by the Allies in early September. Actions later that month included the battle of Flers-Courcelette (the first battle in which tanks were employed), High Wood, Thiepval and Thiepval Ridge.

Battle of the Ancre, November 11-18. The final Somme offensive resulted in the capture by the British of the villages of Beaucourt and Beaumont-Hamel.

An advance of little more than eight miles was made by Haig during the four and a half month period of the battle.

Lloyd George was appointed War Secretary on 6 July owing to Kitchener's death.

The German Command were well aware in the autumn of 1916, of Allied superiority in terms of both men and munitions, and were apprehensive of a renewed Allied offensive on the Somme against exhausted troops so that in mid-September Ludendorff began the construction of the ***Hindenburg Line*** (or the Siegfried Stellurg) – a powerful defence zone some twenty-five miles behind the existing Somme front. (This new shorter front would not be completed until March 1917.)

In Britain, criticism of the Allied conduct of the war as a result of the Somme casualties and Verdun led to the fall of Asquith's coalition government, and Lloyd George being appointed Prime Minister on 7 December. In France, General Joffre was blamed and resigned on 26 December, being replaced by General Robert Nivelle.

1917

Lloyd George was extremely critical of Sir Douglas Haig and his conduct of the war, and committed Britain towards supporting the Nivelle offensive plan for ending the war quickly. Sir Douglas Haig (in charge of British Forces) was subordinated to General Nivelle at the Calais conference on 26 February.

1. On the 16 March, Ludendorff made a massive withdrawal of all German troops to his new strong line of defence the 'Hindenburg Line' thereby straightening out a potentially dangerous Salient The major towns within the areas evacuated by the Germans, such as Bapaume, Peronne and Roye, were abandoned to the Allies, but the area was left as a desert with trees cut down, roads mined, wells fouled, and houses demolished, the ruins being strewn with booby traps.
2. USA enters the war, on 6 April 1917, making the

eventual defeat of Germany possible. There were only 85,000 US troops in France when the Germans launched their last great offensive in March 1918, but there were 1,200,000 there by the following September, under the command of General John Pershing.

3. ***Battle of ARRAS and VIMY RIDGE***, 9 April–17 May. The main role in the British attack fell to the Third Army under Field Marshal Allenby. Further north General Byng's Canadian Corps were to assault the 14 km long Vimy Ridge. The capture of Vimy Ridge was an outstanding triumph for the Canadian Corps. The ridge was a vital part of the German defence system and was so well fortified that all previous attempts to take it by Allied forces had failed. Allenby's attack further south near the River Scarpe was not able to capitalise on initial success and the main offensive came to a close on 14 April, due to the intensity of German counter attacks

4. The disastrous French 'Nivelle' offensive opened on 16 April at the ***Second Battle of the AISNE.*** It aimed to break through the German lines on the Chemin des Dames, between Rheims and Soissons, but completely failed. Mutiny in the French Army resulted in the swift removal of General Nivelle and his replacement on 15 May 1917 by General Petain.

5. ***Battle of MESSINES RIDGE (Ypres)***, 7 June–14 June. Its aim was to flatten out the Salient south of Ypres. Shafts were dug by the Tunnelling Companies over a period of six months, in order to place nineteen mines below the German trenches. They were successfully exploded on 7 June signalling the beginning of the battle of Messines, with a British victory by the Second Army under General Sir H. Plumer, and the final destruction of Hill 60. The effect of the underground explosions was devastating. Within four days the Germans abandoned Messines and Wytschaete and withdrew to a line further east.

6. ***Third Battle of YPRES (Passchendaele)***, 31 July–10 November. A series of separate battles which culminated in the fight for Passchendaele in late October and early November:
Battle of Pilckem, 31 July–2 August
Battle of Langemarck, 16–18 August
Battle of the Menin Road, 20–25 September
Battle of Polygon Wood, 26 September–3 October
Battle of Broodseinde, 4 October
Battle of Poelcappelle, 9 October
First Passchendaele, 12 October
Second Passchendaele, 26 October-10 November.

By the 12 October the Allied forces had made an advance of about five miles from Ypres and secured the main ridges. The village of Passchendaele was taken by the Canadians on 6 November. Casualties on both sides were severe. The Allied dead and wounded numbered almost 245,000. The Germans suffered in the region of 400,000 casualties, and a severe blow to their morale. (Five months later on 15 April 1918, the Passchendaele ridge was retaken by the Germans.)

7. ***Battle of CAMBRAI***, (20 November–3 December) On 20 November an offensive, involving 378 Mark IV tanks, was launched on German positions along a six-mile front by the British Third Army under General Sir Julian Byng. Although a triumph initially with substantial gains, the potential of this successful attack was not exploited. On 30 November the Germans launched a successful counter-attack regaining lost ground and on 3 December the battle finally died down. Each side suffered about 45,000 casualties. The battle of Cambrai was the first time that tanks had been used on a large scale. 56% of the tanks were destroyed or immobilised by the Germans.

1918

1. On 21 March, Ludendorff, using 62 divisions, launched his successful ***Spring SOMME Offensive (code-name 'Michael')*** known as the ***'Kaiserchlacht'*** – the Kaiser's battle.

The 'March Offensive' took the British by surprise and was one of the great dramas of the war. 21 March was a morning of dense fog. At 4.40

a.m. the German forces delivered an immense artillery bombardment. The battle was in many ways a disaster for the British Army, with communications cut and forward troops suddenly involved in retreat. The Germans made the largest territorial gains of the war with an advance of forty miles on a sixty mile front. Paris was bombarded by long range artillery. Albert was taken by the Germans. Ludendorff's last stroke in the offensive was a failure. His attack was abandoned nine miles short of Amiens. On 5 April Ludendorff admitted defeat. Despite a massive retreat Haig's forces were still holding an unbroken line of defence.

Marshal Foch was appointed Allied Commander-in-Chief on 26 March 1918.

2. ***Battle of the LYS (code-name 'Georgette')***, 9–29 April. The second move in Ludendorff's offensive campaign took place in Flanders. The German's achieved a ten mile penetration by 12 April and recaptured the Messines ridge. They mounted a massive gas bombardment on 20 April, south of Ypres, but abandoned the offensive on 29 April.

3. ***Third Battle of the AISNE*** (code-name 'Blucher'), 27 May. Ludendorff's third offensive and a spectacular German victory. After storming the Chemin des Dames ridge in the French sector, the Germans crossed the River Aisne and by 28 May had made an advance of fifteen miles through Allied lines on a twenty-four mile front. German troops entered Soissons on 29 May and by 30 May had reached the River Marne, near Château-Thierry. By 1 June they were forty miles from Paris.

4. ***Second Battle of the MARNE***. The last German offensive began on 14 July near Château Thierry. Both Allied and German forces suffered dreadful carnage. Lack of a decisive breakthrough represented a defeat for Ludendorff, and a turning point in the war.

5. Marshal Foch launches the Allied ***AISNE-MARNE counter-attack*** on 18 July, driving the Western Front eastwards. It began with a 2,000-gun bombardment along a twenty-seven mile front and resulted in an advance of more than four miles into German lines. On 19 July advances by the French and Americans on the Soissons Front led the Germans to abandon Château-Thierry on 21 July, effectively the end of the Marne Salient.

British tanks and troops advance two miles on the Somme Front on 23 July.

6. ***Battle of AMIENS, 8 August–4 September.*** A major Allied victory. Ludendorff wrote 'The 8 August was the black day of the German army in the history of war'. The well planned attack was made by the British Fourth Army under the command of General Rawlinson along a fourteen-mile front. Three hundred and forty-two Mark V tanks were involved and made a big contribution to the victory, despite the fact that by 12 August only six tanks were still available for battle. The town of Albert was recaptured by the British during 21–23 August and Bapaume by the New Zealand division on 29 August. Australian forces gained Peronne on 31 August. The Germans suffered heavy losses and were forced on the 3 September to retire to the Hindenburg Line, finally convincing Ludendorff of the need to end the war. British and French forces at the battle of Epehy (12–15 September), captured a twenty mile long, advanced, fortified zone of the Hindenburg line. Allied strategy in the late summer of 1918 gave the Americans a vital role in operations on the borders of Champagne.

7. ***Battle of ST MIHIEL (south-east of Verdun), 12–16 September.*** An important strategic victory. The St Mihiel Salient, a long-standing threat to any Allied movements in Champagne, was successfully reduced by General Pershing's US First Army together with the French II Colonial Corps. The attack, the first time the Americans went into action on the Western Front as an independent army, was supported by an Allied air force of some 600 planes. Pershing had agreed to attack with the French in the Argonne forest immediately the St Mihiel operation had been concluded. He shifted his entire army of over a million men with tanks and guns by night over some sixty miles with an inadequate road and rail network to the Meuse

valley and Argonne forest area.

8. ***Battle of MEUSE-ARGONNE, 26 September–11 November.*** This involved the American First and the French Fourth Armies. After a preliminary six-hour bombardment more than 700 tanks followed by infantry drove the Germans back three miles. Despite setbacks due to the fierce defence offered by the Germans, the 79th division of the American V Corps took Montfaucon ridge on the 27 September. The First Army continued to batter its way forward in a series of costly attacks. The American First division lost 9,387 men, the heaviest casualties suffered by any US division in the offensive.

9. ***The Second Battle of Cambrai*** and the storming of the Hindenburg Line commenced on 27 September. This highly successful offensive by the British First, Third and Fourth Armies, resulted in large German losses.

10. ***GREAT FLANDERS Offensive (The Fourth Battle of Ypres)***, began on the 28 September. By the 2 October, General Plumer's Second Army together with a Franco-Belgian Army and 500 aircraft had driven a large wedge into German positions – effectively the end of the Ypres Salient. By the 5 October, Allied troops, through the use of integrated artillery and infantry attacks with limited objectives, had smashed gaps right through the Hindenburg Line leaving only sections in German hands. In the British assault on the Sambre Canal on 4 November, Wilfred Owen was hit and killed near the village of Ors. By November about a quarter of the German Army in the field were taken prisoner and half of all its guns captured.

11. ***MONS (Belgium), November 1918.*** The last action on the Western Front was fought at Mons, the scene of the first battle of the First World War in which the BEF were involved. Peace initiatives by Germany lead to the signing of the Armistice on 11 November.

Paris Peace conference, January 1919. German Fleet scuttled at Scapa Flow in the Orkneys, 21 June 1919.

The Treaty of Versailles. On 22 June, the German delegates agreed to sign all the clauses in the peace treaty with the exception of those relating to 'war guilt'. When news of the scuttling of the Fleet at Scapa Flow reached Allied leaders, they decided to reject any alterations in the treaty.

The Treaty of Versailles was signed on 28 June 1919 between Germany and 'The Principal Allied and Associated Powers'. Under the treaty Germany was punished both territorially and financially.

In the latter part of 1918, a devastating pandemic of 'Spanish' Influenza swept the world, causing 20 million deaths. In the American army more soldiers died of influenza (62,000) than were killed in battle. Very heavy casualties were sustained by all the armies involved in the conflict. French dead amounted to 3.5% of the total population; German to 2.9%, and British to 1.9%.

In Britain, as a result of the war, about 9 per cent of males under forty-five years of age were killed.

2
GLOSSARY

Artillery. The essence of trench warfare and the greatest fear of the infantryman. Artillery was classified either by bore diameter (e.g., 77 mm) or weight of shell (e.g., 60 pdr – delivering a 60 lb shell).
Howitzer. A short, squat gun used for shelling at a steep angle, for example, in siege and trench warfare. The German 5.9 inch howitzer was a most effective weapon. The British used a 4.5 inch field howitzer firing a 35 lb shell, and the 9.2 inch heavy howitzer which fired a 290 lb shell. A massive 42 cm howitzer, nicknamed 'Big Bertha', firing a 2,052 lb shell was used by the Germans attacking Liege in 1914.
Field guns. The French 75 mm was the most celebrated field gun of the war, with the fastest rate of firing. The standard British field guns were the Mk 1, 18-pdr and the 60-pdr. The principal German field gun, 77 mm, fired a high velocity 15 lb shell called a 'Whizzbang' by our troops. The artillery also dispensed shrapnel, shells filled with steel balls and a bursting charge and fuse which caused the shell to explode in flight with a resulting hail of metal.

Artois. The territory occupying a chalk plateau between Flanders and Picardy, acquired by France from Spain in 1659, now occupying the department of Pas-de-Calais. Arras lies on the navigable Scarpe river and is the capital of Artois. Ten km north of Arras lies Vimy Ridge, captured by the Canadian Army in 1917.

Augean stable. Abominably filthy, resembling the stable of King Augeus which contained thirty-three oxen and had been uncleansed for thirty years. Hercules by turning the River Alpheus through it purified it in a single day.

Battalion. An establishment of 1,000 men under the command of a Lt-Col.

Casemates. Any bomb-proof vaulted shelter.

Chemical warfare. Chlorine gas, phosgene, and mustard gas, in the form of pressurised liquids were the main gas warfare weapons. Following the Second Battle of Ypres, a 'Special Brigade' made up initially of chemists, and eventually with a strength of just under 6,000, was formed to be responsible for British gas 'retaliation'. Their first gas attack, using chlorine discharged from cylinders, was at Loos in September 1915, but results were disappointing for a number of reasons: the apparatus was cumbersome, faulty cylinders and connecting pipes often leaked and there was the problem of the gas blowing back into British trenches. By mid-1916 the French and Germans had abandoned cylinders using instead gas artillery shells, containing a mixture of chlorine and phosgene. The British continued to use cylinders but in addition developed a Gas mortar projector capable of firing shells of liquefied gas.

Chlorine gas. First used by the Germans on 22 April 1915 near Langemarck in the Ypres Salient. Those badly gassed developed severe inflammation of the lungs. The most authoritative account of chemical warfare dealing with the 1915–1918 period states: 'We shall never know how many were killed by gas, for throughout the war there were no accurate records of those whose death in action was directly attributable to this weapon.' There were approximately 186,000 casualties, of which over 4 per cent were fatal in the BEF. The number of fatalities was greater in the 1915–16 period than in the latter part of the war.

Company. An establishment of 250 men under the command of a Captain.

Enfilade. The discharge of firearms along the whole length of a trench or line of men, rather than crossways.

Fascine. Bundle of sticks or brushwood traditionally used in siegecraft; also carried upon tanks to fill ditches or trenches to allow vehicles to cross.

Five-nine. The British term for a German 5.9 inch shell.

Flame-throwers (Flammenwerfer). Invented in 1900 and used by the Germans for the first time on 26 February 1915 against the French at Verdun, the first of an estimated 653 flame-thrower attacks. The first use against the British was at Hooge (Ypres Salient) in July 1915. A jet of flammable oil ignited by automatic lighters was thrown by means of compressed air, via lengths of steel tubing, to a distance of about twenty-five metres with considerable noise and smoke. The short range was a disadvantage and the teams operating them quickly became exposed to machine-gun fire.

Grenade (British Mills). The later versions of this grenade were the most outstandingly effective trench weapon of the war. Invented by Mr W. Mills of Birmingham (he was knighted after the war), over 75 million were manufactured. They were in use from May 1915 onwards. Activated when a pin was pulled from the grenade, this ignited a delayed explosion. The early versions of the grenade had a five second fuse and a range of about thirty metres. In May 1916 the design was changed slightly so that the grenade had a six second fuse and could be loaded into the muzzle of a rifle and launched by means of a blank cartridge (range seventy-five metres). Owing to the damage caused to the rifles firing the grenades, the design was again changed, resulting in the Hand and Rifle Grenade No 36, in use from late 1917. The German infantryman used a range of grenades. The stick bomb, which could be thrown some distance by means of its wooden handle, was very effective, having a range of about sixty metres.

'Hate'. A bombardment.

Howitzer. See Artillery.

Limber. The detachable forepart of a gun carriage.

Machine-Guns. Bayonets and rifles were the primary weapons of the infantry in 1914, but gradually the machine-gun became dominant, for example, in the Battle of the Somme (1 July 1916). The Germans had been the first to appreciate the importance of the machine-gun in modern warfare and maintained the lead in their use throughout the war. ***The Maxim heavy machine-gun*** (weighing 80 kg), the world's first automatic machine-gun, was invented by American Hiram Maxim and used to great advantage by the German forces. It had a rate of fire of 400–600 rounds per minute The standard machine-gun of the British army was the water-cooled ***Vickers*** weighing 18 kg, a modified version of the Maxim requiring a heavy tripod and water tank to operate. The British also used the portable ***Lewis machine-gun*** (weighing 11.8 kg) invented by American Samuel Maclean and developed by Colonel Isaac Lewis, which first appeared in 1911. It was the first light automatic weapon to be used on a large scale and was in use during the Second World War.

'Minenwerfer' (mine-thrower). A type of German trench mortar firing a missile weighing around 90 kg and exploding with a tremendous roar – referred to as 'Moaning Minnies'.

Mortars. Various devices were used for hurling bombs into enemy trenches. The early trench mortar bombs were known as 'Toffee Apples' or 'Plum Puddings'. By early 1915 two heavy mortars were in use by the British (the 4 inch and the 3. 7 inch), plus a light mortar, the 2 inch. A portable mortar was required and Wilfred Stokes, the manager of a light engineering firm, Ransome and Rapier, was entrusted with its development. Due to initial problems, Stokes withdrew to his cottage at Ripley in Surrey, to improve the design of the shell. He changed the cylindrical shape to a streamlined one and decided to use ballistite (invented by Nobel) as a propellant. Eventually the ***Stokes Mortar*** went into service at the end of March 1916. It was portable and a most effective weapon, a kind of pocket artillery.

Mustard Gas (Dichlordiethyl sulphide). Introduced in 1917 at Ypres and therefore also known as 'Yperite'. Responsible for most of the gas casualties between autumn 1917, and the end of the war. It had a delayed effect, two or three hours after exposure, causing flu-like symptoms, painful blistering of the skin and sometimes pneumonia. It was first used at the Third Battle of Ypres (Passchendaele) and caused 2,100 casualties in the British sector, fifty to sixty of which were fatal. Due to delays in manufacture, sufficient stocks of mustard gas were not available for use by the British until the end of September 1918.

Parados. The side of a trench farthest from the enemy.

Parapets. The side of a trench facing the enemy.

Phosgene gas (Carbonyl chloride). Phosgene was introduced in December 1915 and used by both the Germans and the British. Ten times more toxic than chlorine it is particularly dangerous due to its delayed action. The British used a 50:50 mixture of chlorine and phosgene (known as 'White Star') as the main filling for gas cylinders from late January 1916 onwards.

Picardy. The region between Paris and Artois composed of sweeping chalk plateaux drained by the Aisne, Oise and Somme rivers. Amiens is the largest town in Picardy.

Plan 17. France's war blueprint, formulated by Marshal Joffre. A French force together with the BEF would move into Belgium if Germany violated that country's neutrality, which it did. The other main thrust was to be into Alsace-Lorraine.

Poilu. French slang for a soldier especially for a front line infantryman.

QAIMNS. Queen Alexandra's Imperial Military Nursing Service.

Rifle, Lee Enfield (.303). The British Service Rifle. Bolt action with a ten-round magazine and a short (25 inch) barrel. Probably the best standard service weapon issued during the war. It required frequent cleaning to operate effectively.

Salient. A trench system projecting towards the enemy. The British position at Ypres was universally known as 'The Salient'.

Schlieffen Plan. Germany's war blueprint, to sweep through Belgium into northern France and crush the French armies west of Paris. The plan was developed by the Chief of the German General Staff (from 1890–1905), Graf Schlieffen.

Shell-shock. A term used for cases of war neurosis in the mistaken belief that shell fire was mainly responsible. Officers were twice as likely as other ranks to suffer mental breakdown. War neurosis involved a psychological collapse caused by prolonged exposure to combat. (The condition is now known as post-traumatic stress disorder/ syndrome.) Some 80,000 'shell-shock' cases passed through army hospitals during the war.

Tear Gas. An irritant type of chemical weapon, for example, ethyl iodoacetate, causing the eyes to water. Temporarily incapacitating.

Traverses. Protrusions of earth or sandbags built into a trench to limit the effects of shells etc.

Western Front. The label applied by the Germans to their front in the west, crossing France and Belgium, as opposed to their eastern front against Russia. More precisely it refers to the battle line which by 1915 stretched for more than four hundred miles, in an unbroken line of trenches and barbed wire, from the Belgian coast (near Ostend) to the Swiss border near Belfort.

3

MILITARY PERSONALITIES OF THE FIRST WORLD WAR

FIELD MARSHAL ALLENBY. 1ST VISCOUNT (1861–1936)

A man of great integrity, 'Bull' Allenby commanded the Third Army of the BEF from October 1915–17 in a competent manner. Allenby and Haig shared a mutual dislike. He achieved his high reputation when after appointment as Commander-in-Chief, Egypt in 1917, he won a series of victories in Palestine. After the war he presided as High Commissioner of Egypt over its attainment of independence.

GENERAL SIR JULIAN BYNG (1862–1935)

One of the better generals of the war. In May 1916 he was given command of the Canadian Corps which he led with distinction for more than a year. Their successes included the capture of Vimy Ridge. His troops became known as 'Byng's Boys', their success possibly due to a more flexible attitude and a closer relationship between the leaders and the led than was often the case in the British Army. Ellison's diary entry for 5 June 1915 certainly supports this view. In June 1917 Byng assumed command of the Third Army leading it with considerable success. He was rewarded after the war with a peerage, Viscount Byng of Vimy, and the post of Governor-General of Canada from 1921–26.

MARSHAL FOCH (1851–1929)

One of the great Commanders of the First World War. He was appointed as Allied Commander-in-Chief on 14 April 1917, and conducted the final offensive, with the British, against the Germans which ended the war. He profoundly influenced military thought in France especially through his book *Principles of War.* He was appointed a British Field Marshal.

FIELD MARSHAL SIR JOHN FRENCH. FIRST EARL OF YPRES (1852–1925)

The First Commander of the BEF. His poor judgement at Ypres and Loos caused his replacement by his Deputy Sir D. Haig in December 1915. He became Commander-in-Chief of Home forces until early 1918, when he was appointed Lord Lieutenant of Ireland.

GENERAL SIR HUBERT GOUGH (1870–1963)

General Sir H. Gough achieved a reputation for being rather careless and disregarding the lives of his soldiers. He owed his rise – and eventual fall – to Haig's favour. Commanding the Fifth Army 1916–18, Gough was chosen by Haig to lead the attack at Passchendaele in July 1917. His attacks achieved nothing except large casualties, and Plumer's Second Army was ordered to take over. When Ludendorff launched his Spring Somme Offensive in March 1918, the Fifth Army was forced to retreat. Because of the *débâcle* Haig decided to put the official blame on Gough for the defeat and he was removed from command. Haig told one of Gough's staff officers: 'After considerable thought, I decided that public opinion at home, rightly or wrong, demanded a scapegoat and that the only possible ones were Hubert and me. I was conceited enough to think that the Army could not spare me.'

SIR DOUGLAS HAIG (1861–1928)

He replaced Sir John French as Commander-in-Chief, BEF in December 1915, until the end of the war in 1918. Lloyd George was very critical of Haig, who was largely responsible for the attritional battle of the Somme. As a result Haig suffered the indignity of being subordinated by Lloyd George to France's General Nivelle at the Calais conference in February 1917. Haig lost further credibility with his conduct of Passchendaele later that year, although it was by Lloyd George's own authorisation that the campaign continued for a month after he had recognised that it could not succeed. Haig lacked the vital quality of imagination and ability to surprise the enemy (qualities possessed by Sir William Plumer). He worked well with Marshal Foch in 1918 when Lloyd George placed British forces under French overall command. Never regarded as a great General, Winston Churchill said: 'He might be, he surely was, unequal to the prodigious scale of events; but no one else was discerned as his equal or better.'

THE HINDENBURG–LUDENDORFF PARTNERSHIP

General Erich von Ludendorff (1865–1937) possessed great strategic skills. He was appointed Field Marshal Paul von Hindenburg's Chief of Staff in 1914. With Hindenburg began the most important partnership of the war, although Ludendorff can be considered to have been the main controller. However, he lacked political vision and after the war became involved with the Nazis. He was a willing accomplice in the promotion of Adolf Hitler to dictator of Germany, and the dissolution of the Weimar Republic.

MARSHAL JOFFRE (1852–1931)

The dominant character in the French military in the first part of the war. He formulated Plan VII, France's war blueprint. He was virtually Allied Commander-in-Chief (although he never held such a title) until he was removed in December 1916 from his post of French Commander-in-Chief and replaced by General Nivelle.

FIELD MARSHAL KITCHENER OF KHARTOUM (1850–1916)

Very successful in recruiting the new British 'Kitchener's Armies' and in establishing a close relationship with France. Appointed Secretary of State for War he ran the British war effort for the first year and a half. Kitchener was basically a one-man show. He was difficult to work with, and by 1915 his influence had declined due to successive military defeats, and the repudiation of his leadership in the Cabinet. Lloyd George developed a particular dislike for Kitchener and tried to drive him out of the War Office. In June 1916 he was drowned when the *Hampshire* taking him on a mission to Russia struck a mine and sank off the Orkneys in June 1916.

GENERAL SIR JOHN MONASH (1865–1931)

Recognised as one of the outstanding Generals of the First World War he was noted for the brilliant planning of his operations. Born in Melbourne, he commanded the 4th Australian Infantry Brigade at Gallipoli in 1915 and the 3rd Australian division at Messines. The Anzacs played an important part in Passchendaele, particularly the battle of Broodseinde on 4 October 1917. He was appointed Commander of the Australian Army Corps making a notable contribution to the Allied victory at the Battle of Amiens in August 1918.

GENERAL NIVELLE (1856–1924)

Responsible for the disastrous 'Nivelle offensive' at the Second Battle of the Aisne in April 1917. The resulting heavy losses and mutinies in the French Army led to his removal in May 1917 and replacement by General Petain.

GENERAL JOHN PERSHING (1860–1948)

Commander of the American Expeditionary Forces which, in 1918 at the battles of St Mihiel and Meuse-Argonne, played a vital role in the final Allied victory. The slow build-up of American troops in France caused a late entry (May 1918) into the war. Pershing was determined to keep the American Army as a separate force and Marshal Foch was eventually forced to give in after acrimonious discussions. Pershing in return committed the American First Army to the September offensives at St Mihiel and Meuse-Argonne. After the war he became Chief of Staff of the United States army (1921–24)

GENERAL PETAIN (1856–1951)

He rebuilt morale in the French Army after the Nivelle offensive and the resulting mutinies. He made a large contribution to the success of the war and was appointed Marshal of France in December 1918. His collaboration with the Nazis during the Second World War and the establishment of the Vichy Government resulted in his being condemned to death, although he was reprieved.

FIELD MARSHAL HERBERT PLUMER (1ST VISCOUNT PLUMER) (1857–1932)

Herbert Plumer was undoubtedly one of the best Generals of the war, being completely unflappable. He understood 'siege' warfare and commanded the Second Army which held the Ypres front for two years. He replaced Sir H. Smith-Dorrien who was relieved of his command at Ypres by Sir J. French.

GENERAL HENRY RAWLINSON (1ST BARON) (1864–1925)

Despite a sequence of disastrous battles in 1915, Rawlinson was promoted rapidly and reached Fourth Army command early in 1916. His greatest achievement was the Allied victory at the Battle of Amiens in August 1918.

SIR HORACE SMITH-DORRIEN (1858–1930)

Potentially a great General although he was never able to prove it conclusively. He halted the Allied retreat at Le Cateau in August 1914. Unfortunately he was dismissed from his command of the Second Army at Ypres in April 1915, due to a difference of opinion with Sir J. French (see page 52). French's own study of his BEF command '1914' is to some extent, due to its inaccuracies, a self-justification at the expense of Smith-Dorrien.

SIR WILLIAM ROBERTSON (1860–1933)

He rose from the ranks to become Chief of Imperial General Staff in 1915. However, he came into political disagreement with Lloyd George, and it was for this reason, rather than for any inability, that he was dismissed in February 1918.

4
CAPTAIN BRUCE BAIRNSFATHER AND NATHANIEL GUBBINS, A WAR CARTOONIST AND A JOURNALIST EXTRAORDINAIRE

CAPTAIN BRUCE BAIRNSFATHER (1888–1959)

Foremost of the war cartoonists, Bruce Bairnsfather was born in India. He served with the Royal Warwickshire Regiment from the beginning of the Western Front campaign in November 1914. His first cartoon 'Where did that one go?' was immediately accepted for publication by the *Bystander* magazine, who continued to publish his work, for example, 'Fragments from France' and 'More Fragments from France'. These were a great morale booster to both the troops and civilians. His creation 'Old Bill' and his two mates brought him worldwide fame. He was wounded at the second battle of Ypres and when he recovered returned to the Western Front as the first officially appointed British Officer Cartoonist.

Toni and Valmai Holt believe that the 'Letters From the Front' cartoon included in the Diary was drawn specially for Norman Ellison. This is certainly the case regarding the sketch of 'Old Bill'.

References

Bruce Bairnsfather, *Bullets and Billets* (Grant Richard's Ltd, 1916)
Toni and Valmai Holt, *In Search of the Better 'Ole* (Milestone Publications, 1985. Biography)

'The humorous drawings of Bruce Bairnsfather were one of the good things produced by the War. They boosted civilian morale; the troops loved them. He drew this picture of "Old Bill" for me on the 26 August 1938, when he was playing in his show of that name at the Argyle Theatre, Birkenhead.'

NATHANIEL GUBBINS (1893–1976)

Norman Ellison and Nathaniel Gubbins became friends whilst they were both in the Marlborough Convalescent Camp, near Boulogne in April 1915 (see page 57). Gubbins was a private in the 20th London Regt. He replied to a letter from Ellison after the war in 1930:

Sunday Express Office,
8 Shoe Lane,

11th December 1930

Dear Ellison,

Thanks so much for your letter. I am the identical gnome you met in France in 1915 as a private soldier in the 20th London Regiment and I am extremely glad to hear from you.

'I remember you well in spite of your unflattering description of yourself'. I went home to England shortly after the digging (and bath) incidents and did not go out again.

But they kept me on as a private soldier (and eventually a paid L/Cpl) until the bitter end.

During that time I got into clink, became a musketry instructor and generally made an idiot of myself. If you ever come to London I should be awfully glad to see you. It is a curious thing that I have often remembered you, apart from your letter.

Yours very sincerely,
Nathaniel Gubbins.

Later, after the war, Nat Gubbins became famous as a *Sunday Express* columnist (from 1930–53).

His first column included a brief biographical sketch:

I am about 5ft 10 inches tall, weigh 13 stone and don't look a day over ninety at six o'clock in the morning. I hate regular meals, musical comedies, vivacious women, stewed steak and Christmas. I love cats, pickled onions, cheese, a day in bed, London, more pickled onions, more cheese, another day in bed and kittens.

In *Sitting on the Fence* he contributed an imaginary obituary of himself from *The Times* of 7 April 1953 (which strangely was to be the year he was sacked from the *Sunday Express* by Lord Beaverbrook). He mentions that his military career was an unhappy experience:

He seems to have spent the greater part of his time doing the wrong things and losing equipment, his most vivid experience being the dropping of a tray in the officers' mess and smashing most of the crockery, and losing his rifle at Bethune while on active service. He often said that he was glad he was invalided home early from France because (a) he did not like the war very much and (b) the fact that he took no further part in it, except on home service, may have been a contributing factor to our final victory.

The obituary concludes:

He had no hobbies except listening enraptured to four-ale-bar conversations and collected nothing, not even money. His one violent passion was his hatred of work of any description. He disliked all dogs, loved all cats and was a fool at games. Although his death is no loss to literature, it may cause some temporary inconvenience in Fleet Street, and his friends in various taverns will miss him for at least a week.

References

Nathaniel Gubbins, *Sitting on the Fence* (Anthology introduced by Leonard Russell) (Penguin, 1944).

Godfrey Smith, *The Best of Nathaniel Gubbins* (Blond and Briggs, 1978)

5

THE KING'S LIVERPOOL REGIMENT – 1ST/6TH (RIFLE) BATTALION TERRITORIAL FORCE

MOVEMENTS AND BATTLES

Autumn 1914. Princes Park Barracks, Liverpool to Canterbury.

25 February 1915. Landed at Le Havre. Travelled to Bailleul (to 15 Bde 5 Div).

17 April–1 May 1915. Battle. Capture of Hill 60, Ypres.

18 November 1915. To Third Army Troops.

26 January 1916. To 165 Bde 55 Division.

4 April–28 September 1916. Battles. Somme, Guillemont, Ginchy, Flers-Courcelette, Morval.

31 July–3 December 1917. Battles. Ypres, Pilckem Ridge, Menin Road Ridge, Cambrai.

9 April–11 November 1918. Battles. Lys, Estairs, Givenchy, Hazebrouck, Givenchy Craters, Canteleux Trench, Artois, Mons.

11 November 1918. Belgium-West of Ath.

'A SHORT HISTORY'

The following letter appeared in the *Liverpool Echo* on 25 November 1927:

> I am sure that many ex-service men among your readers will be interested to know that it is proposed to bring out a short history of the 6th Rifle Battalion, the King's Regiment, Liverpool.
>
> While endeavouring to produce an accurate account of the battalion's part in the late war, it will be the aim of the compilers to embody as much material as possible, gathered from the personal experiences of all ranks, and to avoid a mere dry recitation of events, by introducing those human elements which alone maintain the interest of old members of the battalion, no less than that of the general reader.
>
> Would those who served in the battalion during the war and who would be prepared to lend any personal diary, or give any account of particular experiences, please send their names and addresses to either Colonel J.B. McKaig, DSO, TD, DL, 18, Sefton Drive, Liverpool; or Mr N.F. Ellison, 5 Parkfield Drive, Wallasey.

Norman Ellison writes:

> The above letter brought several letters and diaries. I had written some 40,000 words covering the record of the battalion before approaching Colonel McKaig with the manuscript. He approved of it as did Colonel Harrison and Major Glyn Blackedge who had started a short history in the official organ of the battalion *The Green Jacket*. Finance was necessary to pay the printers etc, but although the Officers' Association had ample funds, they hummed and harred for years until at last I gave up trying to obtain a definite decision from them. The many hours I had spent in getting material were not wasted – much of the material I have used in this book.

References

Lt-Col J.J. Burke-Gaffney, MC, *The Story of the King's Regiment* (Sharpe and Kellet, 1954)

The History of the King's Regiment (Liverpool) Three volumes: volume 1 (1914–1915); volume 2 (1916–1917); volume 3 (1917–1919). (Edward Arnold, 1925–35. Completed by Captain W.A.T. Synge)

Graham Maddocks, *Liverpool Pals.* A History of the 17th, 18th, 19th and 20th Service Battalions, the King's (Liverpool Regiment), 1914–1919 (Leo Cooper, 1991)

T.R. Threlfall, *The Story of the King's (Liverpool Regiment)* (Country Life Library, 1916. Preface by Lord Derby)

Ray Westlake, *British Battalions on the Somme* (Leo Cooper, 1994)

BIBLIOGRAPHY AND FURTHER READING

The books listed represent a personal choice from the literature on the First World War. The editor and publisher gratefully acknowledge the source works that provide the context for the Ellison diary.

Robert Graves captures the reality of war in his autobiographical *Goodbye to All That*, despite the fact that Edmund Blunden and S. Sassoon were so incensed by Graves's book (which they regarded as inaccurate) that they subtitled it 'The Welsh-Irish Bull in a China Shop'.

The War the Infantry Knew by Captain J.C. Dunn (published originally in 1938) is an outstanding account of an infantry battalion's experience on the Western Front. Sir Philip Gibbs achieved a great reputation as a War Correspondent. Of his many books *Realities of War* and *The War Dispatches* are particularly recommended. Modern classics include *Some Desperate Glory* by Edwin Campion Vaughan, and *The Price of Glory. Verdun 1916* by Alistair Horne.

The First World War 1914–1918 by John Terraine succeeds in its aim of clarifying the many complexities of the war. Martin Gilbert's *The First World War* and *Facing Armageddon. The First World War Experienced*, edited by Hugh Cecil and Peter Liddle, are excellent recent works. *Before Endeavours Fade* by Rose E.B. Coombs is a classic guide to the battlefields of the Western Front. For a military history of northern France and southern Belgium *The Fatal Avenue* by Richard Holmes is of particular value.

Bernard Adams, *Nothing of Importance* (Reissued by Strong Oak Press & Tom Donovan Publishing, 1988. First published 1917)

Robert. B. Asprey, The *German High Command at War. Hindenburg and Ludendorff and the First World War* (Little Brown and Co, 1993)

Correlli Barnett, *The Sword-bearers. Studies in Supreme Command in the First World War* (Eyre & Spottiswoode, 1963)

Alexander Barrie, *War Underground. The Tunnellers of the Great War* (Tom Donovan, 1962. Reprint 1993)

Edmund Blunden, *Undertones of War* (First published in 1928. Penguin Modern Classics, 1982. Folio Society, 1989)

Beatrix Brice, *The Battle Book of Ypres* (John Murray, 1987. First published 1927)

Adrian Bristow, *A Serious Disappointment. The Battle of Aubers Ridge*, 1915 (Leo Cooper, 1995)

Guy Chapman, *A Passionate Prodigality* (First published by Ivor Nicholson and Watson Ltd, 1933. Second edition, McGibbon and Kee Ltd, 1965. Reprint by Ashford, Buchan and Enright, 1990. (Note: The autobiography of Guy Chapman, *A Kind of Survivor*, edited by his widow, Storm Jameson, was published by Gollancz, 1975.))

Winston S. Churchill, *The World Crisis 1916–1918* (Thornton Butterworth, 1927)

Alan Clark, *The Donkeys* (Pimlico, 1991. Hutchinson, 1961)

Rose E.B. Coombs, *Before Endeavours Fade* (Battle of Britain International, 1986)

Jilly Cooper, *Animals in War* (Published for the trustees of the Imperial War Musuem by W. Heinemann Ltd, 1983)

Captain J.C Dunn, *The War the Infantry Knew*, 1914–1919 (Abacus Books, 1994. First published by P.S. King Ltd, 1938 in a private edition of 500 copies)

Field Marshal Vicount French *1914* (Constable, 1919)

Paul Fussell, *The Great War and Modern Memory* (Oxford University Press, 1975: paperback, 1977)

John Giles, *Flanders Then and Now. The Ypres Salient and Passchendaele* (Revised edition Battle of Britain Prints International Ltd, 1987)
The Somme Then and Now (Picardy Publishing, 1986)
The Western Front Then and Now (Battle of Britain Prints International Ltd, 1992)

Martin Gilbert, *The First World War* (Weidenfeld and Nicolson, 1994)

General Sir Hubert Gough, *The Fifth Army* (Hodder and Stoughton, 1931)
Soldiering On (Arthur Barker, 1954)

Richard Perceval Graves, *Robert Graves. The Assault Heroic 1895–1926* (Weidenfeld and Nicolson, 1986: paperback, 1995)

Robert Graves, *Goodbye to All That* (Revised edition, Cassell, 1957. First and second edition, Jonathan Cape, 1929)

Guy Hartcup, *The War of Invention*. Scientific Developments, 1914–18 (Brassey Defence Publishers Ltd, 1988)

Philip J. Haythornthwaite, *The World War One Source Book* (Cassell, Arms and Armour Press, 1992)

Richard Holmes, *Fatal Avenue* A Traveller's History of the battlefields of Northern France and Flanders, (1346–1945) (J. Cape, 1992)

Richard Holmes *Riding the Retreat. Mons to the Marne, 1914.* (J. Cape, 1995. Pimlico paperback, 1996)

Alistair Horne, *The Price of Glory. Verdun 1916* (Penguin, 1983. Macmillan, 1962)

Lawrence James, *Imperial Warrior. The Life and Times of Field Marshal Viscount Allenby* (Weidenfeld and Nicolson, 1993)

Peter H. Liddle, *The Soldier's War 1914–1918* (Blandford Press, 1988)
The 1916 Battle of the Somme. A Reappraisal (Leo Cooper, 1992)
Facing Armageddon. The First World War Experienced (Leo Cooper, 1996. Edited by Hugh Cecil and Peter Liddle)

B.H. Liddell Hart, *History of the First World War* (Cassell, 1970)

Oliver Lyttleton (Viscount Chandos) *From Peace to War. A Study in Contrast 1857–1918*. (Bodley Head, 1968).

Lyn Macdonald *1915 The Death of Innocence* (Hodder Headline, 1993).

General Sir James Marshall-Cornwall. *Foch as Military Commander* (B.T. Batsford Ltd, 1972).

Martin Middlebrook, *The First Day on the Somme* (Allen Lane, 1971)

Robin Prior and Trevor Wilson, *Passchendaele. The Untold Story* (Yale University Press, 1996)

Sidney Rogerson, *Twelve Days. The Somme 1916.* (First published 1930 by Arthur Barker Ltd.

Reissued by Gliddon Books, 1988).

Peter Simkins, *Kitchener's Army. The Raising of the New Armies, 1914–16* (Manchester University Press, 1988)

A.J. Smithers, *The Man Who Disobeyed. Sir Horace Smith-Dorrien & His Enemies* (Leo Cooper, 1970)

Major-General Sir Edward Spears, *Prelude to Victory* (Jonathan Cape, 1939)

Rev G.A. Studdert Kennedy *The Hardest Part.* (Hodder and Stoughton, 1919)

John Terraine, *Mons. The Retreat to Victory* (Leo Cooper, 1991. Batsford, 1960)
Douglas Haig: *The Educated Soldier* (Hutchinson, 1963)
The First World War 1914–1918. (Macmillian, 1965. New edition. Sechard Warling, 1983).
The Smoke and the Fire. Myths and Anti-Myths of War (Sidgwick & Jackson, 1980)

Edwin Campion Vaughan, *Some Desperate Glory* (Leo Cooper in association with F. Warne Ltd, 1981)

Jeffrey Williams, *Byng of Vimy.* General and Governor-General. (Leo Cooper, 1983 and 1992)

Leon Wolff, *In Flanders Fields. The 1917 Campaign* (Longmans, Green and Co, 1958)

NORMAN ELLISON BIBLIOGRAPHY

Down Nature's Byways Illustrations by Alfred Preston 1938

Wandering with Nomad (1946)

Out of Doors with Nomad (1947)

Over the Hills with Nomad (1948)

Roving with Nomad (1949)

Adventuring with Nomad (1950)

Northwards with Nomad (1951)

(All the 'Nomad' books were illustrated by C.F. Tunnicliffe and published by University of London Press.)

British Birds and Beasts, N.F. Ellison with photographs by Eric Hosking and illustrations by A.K. Wiffen (Countrygoer Books, 1947)

The Wirral Peninsula (Robert Hale, 1955)

George Ellison, Naturalist Chronicler of the Orkneys, North Western Naturalist, Volume XIX (1944-45) (Article by N.F. Ellison regarding his Uncle)

MEMOIRS

Norman Ellison memoirs (18 volumes), plus other material, held by the Liverpool Record Office, Central Library.

1. Early Days, 1893–1914.
2. War Diary, 1914–1919.
3. The Approaching Storm, 1919–1938.
4. War on the Home Front, 1939–1945.
5. Outdoors with Nomad, 1946–1949.
6. Nomad Not Out 150, 1950–1955.
7. Liverpool My City, 1956–1960.
8. The Sensational Sixties, 1961–1964.
9. Curiouser and Curiouser, 1965.
10. Now Comes the Reckoning, 1966.
11. Confusion Worse Confounded, 1967.
12. Wirral – God's Croft, 1968.
13. Target Moon, 1969.
14. I Remember, I Remember, 1970.
15. The Measure of the Year, 1971.
16. And Then to Thinking, 1972, 1973 (Jan–June).
17. Through the Motley Rout, 1973 (July–December), 1974.
18. Volume 18, Memoirs, 1975. Unbound.

    Two bound volumes of Letters to N. Ellison, responding to his request for advice regarding his *War Diary, 1914–1919.*

    Four volumes of the Minutes of 'The Old Insufferables'.

THE BBC SOUND ARCHIVE

The following are the only three recordings of the 'Nomad' programmes that exist in the BBC Sound Archive:

Wandering with Nomad, No 146, Children's Hour, 30 June 1953 (ICE 0001319)

Nomad Visit to Hilbre Island. Northern Naturalist, 27 March 1956 (LP 23236)

Wandering with Nomad. A Visit to Bird Island, 11 May 1961 (LP 26979)

These recordings are BBC copyright but available for listening at the National Sound Archive, 29, Exhibition Road, London SW7 2AS, provided that notice is given.

INDEX